POCKET
DAD

Library of Congress Cataloging in
Publication Number: 2005935312

ISBN: 1-59474-092-5

Printed in Malaysia

Typeset in Bembo, Franklin Gothic, and SignPainter

Designed by Doogie Horner

Illustrations by Mark Harfield

Distributed in North America by Chronicle Books
85 Second Street
San Francisco, CA 94105

10 9 8 7 6 5 4 3 2 1

Quirk Books
215 Church Street
Philadelphia, PA 19106
www.quirkbooks.com

POCKET DAD

EVERYDAY WISDOM, PRACTICAL TIPS, AND FATHERLY ADVICE

BY DINA FAYER AND BOB FAYER

QUIRK BOOKS

PHILADELPHIA

Contents

Chapter 1: The Essential Dad

Chapter 2: Handyman Dad

Chapter 3: Dad in the Driver's Seat

Chapter 4: Dad in the Great Outdoors

Chapter 5: Dad on the Home Front

Chapter 6: Dad on Success

Introduction

When your sump pump goes thump, you call a plumber. When your finances get tangled, you phone the appropriate bean counter. Car won't start? You find a mechanic. Well, that's all very sensible (and oh so independent)—but wouldn't it be simpler if you just asked Dad?

Dad is all the best parts of the yellow pages rolled into one—and more! Dad is a multipurpose multitasker: Whenever he isn't fixing what's broken, he becomes a world-class snowman builder, tie tier, advice giver, and yarn spinner extraordinaire. If there's something in your life that Dad doesn't have an opinion on, you have yet to meet it.

Where does he get this stuff? Dead knights from the Middle Ages? Ancient detective shows? Or (heaven forbid!) *his* dad? Wherever it comes from, the unabridged, annotated gospel of Dad could fill several bookshelves and more than one brain. In essence, he's the Swiss Army Dad—you'd fold him up and put him in your pocket every day, if you could.

And now, of course, you can, with *Pocket Dad*. This field guide to "Life as Dad Sees It" will give you the most vital how-to details on everything from changing a tire to changing a prospective employer's mind to becoming a happy, responsible adult by rediscovering your inner goofiness. Wherever life takes you, Dad will never steer you wrong. Just don't forget to wear your seat belt!

CHAPTER 1:
The Essential Dad

It never rains on Dad's parade.

Come to think of it, when's the last time you've seen a parade . . . or visited the zoo . . . or told an awful joke and felt pride when someone slugged you for it? If you haven't been a child since your childhood ended, it's time to revisit some of Dad's favorite lessons.

Dad knows—better than anyone else—how to get the most fun out of virtually any situation. He's the perfect antidote to boredom. His Dad-tastic antics could turn the agony of long car trips, bad weather, slow restaurants, and even family reunions into good times.

Whistle While You Work

 You know how to whistle, don't you? If not, it's time to learn.

There are all kinds of ways you can whistle—including through your nose—but for entertainment value when you're on a long road trip, the pucker can't be beat.

DAD SAYS: "Learn to carry a tune, and you'll take it with you everywhere."

1. Pucker your lips. Your top and bottom lips should be equally pursed and open just enough to admit a plastic straw.

2. Arch your tongue. Press the back of your tongue to your top molars and the tip of your tongue to the floor of your mouth, pushing down and forward. In the proper position, your tongue will fill the entire width of your mouth.

3. Keep your tongue in this position, and breathe in and out through your mouth a few times. The air should make a whistling sound.

4. Once your tongue discovers the basic whistle position, the rest is fine-tuning. More air, expelled with more force, increases volume. Squish your tongue forward and backward, and you'll succeed in changing your pitch: Higher notes are produced by pushing your tongue forward, while low notes are made by retracting it.

5. If the process feels awkward, you're trying too hard to control the mechanics. Concentrate on your breathing, and do your best rendition of your favorite melody.

The Box Step: As Easy as One-Two-Three

 The best way to learn to dance is to step outside the box.

Chances are, you've already learned the box step from Dad, Mom, some aunts, and a teacher. But it never stuck—so what gives? That's because the box step done slowly, with fixed eyes and dilated pupils, bears little resemblance to the actual waltz. Without that regular one-two-three rhythm, the dance is just an unnatural lurch.

DAD SAYS: "Forget what your feet are *supposed* to be doing, and get used to moving in three-quarter time."

1. Familiarize yourself with waltz tempos. Put on a good Strauss CD, and tap your foot in time for a while.

2. Stand in one place, and shift your weight from foot to foot in time with the music. Right-left-right. Left-right-left. And so on.

3. Once you've got the hang of the rhythm, start moving around the room. Don't worry about the steps. Waltz to the fridge to get a soda. Waltz to the bathroom. If you're feeling daring, try a turn.

4. Now, you're ready for the box step: Forward with your left foot,

forward/right with your right foot, then meet your right foot when you step with your left.

5. The next three steps will be backward, as your partner steps forward. Forward set, backward set. Forward set, backward set. Don't look at your feet!

6. Practice with a partner privately. Nothing takes the wind out of your sails like public humiliation, so you'll want to avoid that.

7. When the time is right, go out on the town. See where your smooth moves take you.

Happiness Is Building a Snowman

 Perfect snowmen are built, not born.

When's the last time you headed out to the wilds of your own front yard, squatting for hours in subarctic temperatures because snow was fun? Stop shoveling snow off that driveway, and sculpt an old friend instead.

DAD SAYS: "Start with the right kind of snow."

1. The snow should be dry enough to pack, and not too powdery. There should also be enough of it to go around. A snowman with a mud superstructure will likely become nothing more than a mudman by the time you're finished.

2. Collect a good-sized ball of snow in both hands. Roll it across the ground, scooping more snow onto the ball and packing it down with your hands. Keep rolling and

packing until it's big enough to serve as the base, or body, of the figure.

3. Repeat the process with two successively smaller balls, stacking them up to create a torso and a head. If you really want your snowman to last, try linking the balls of snow with sticks or small branches, to give it some support.

4. Use branches to fashion snowman arms and legs. Simply insert two branches of roughly the same size into the snow torso, then insert branch legs into the lower body.

5. Put on your snow face: insert pebbles for eyes and mouth—and use the old traditional carrot for a nose.

6. Once the basic shape is in place, you can really have fun. Dress up your snowman like the nuisancy neighbor next door, or put it in an old fake fur coat and call it Abominable. Or better yet, paint it with food coloring in water, and call it anything you want.

Sculpt a Sand Castle Masterpiece

Low tide is the best time to build sand castles, because there's plenty of moist, workable sand that isn't about to be swamped by a wave. You'll have plenty of time to measure, design, and produce your masterpiece before the sea pours in to claim it.

DAD SAYS: "Get off your towel, and go play in the sand."

1. Use ingenuity to select your tools. "Tools" are any hollow items (empty coolers work best for the bases of buildings; disposable cups are best for towers) that can be filled with packed sand and used to cast campaniles, turrets, and other structural elements. Plastic shovels are perfect for excavations.

2. Comb the beach for additional implements. You'll need a sharp stick to draw in the details, plus shells, rocks, and any other bits that look decorative or useful to your eye.

3. Set the perimeter of your castle. Determine how much space your castle will occupy, and mark it out by drawing a trench with your stick. This will help you remember where not to step as you begin to erect towers and battlements.

4. Enlist the help of buddies, children, and other beachgoers to construct your base. As you move

on to the narrow towers, winnow down your help to only the experienced castle builders.

5. Use your tools to cut in windows and embellishments.

6. Dig a trench around the castle to serve as your moat.

7. Sit back and enjoy the admiration of passersby—and let the sea take care of the rest.

 Tip Never deconstruct. If you aren't happy with the progress of your castle, make do with what you have and improvise as you build upward. Remember, you only have until the tide comes in to build a whole castle.

Bad Dad Jokes for Beginners

 Comedy is all about delivery.

Dad's a funny guy, but his jokes are awful. And the worse they get, the more he laughs. Here are a few of his best worst gems. Tell these jokes as if they were funny, and you'll be surprised by the laughs you get.

DAD SAYS: "The best laughs come when you're laughing at yourself."

Snoo.

Dad: Hey, you got any snoo?

You: What's snoo?

Dad: Not much, what's new with you?

Machine

Dad: How do you pronounce the word M-a-c-G-u-i-r-e?

You: MacGuire.

Dad: How do you pronounce the word M-a-c-L-e-a-n?

You: MacLean.

Dad: How do you pronounce the word M-a-c-H-i-n-e?

You: MacHine.

Dad: Hee, hee, hee [wipes his eyes]. You can't say the word *machine!*

Cheese

What do you call someone else's cheese? Nacho cheese.

Dead Parrot

A woman rushes into the vet's office holding a limp parrot. "There's something wrong with my bird!" she cries. The vet takes one look at the parrot and says, "I'm very sorry, but your parrot is dead." The woman can't believe it. "You didn't even examine him," she protests. "You didn't do any tests!"

The vet shrugs and nods and lifts a cat up next to the bird. The cat pokes it and bats it with his paw and shakes his head. Next, the vet invites a chocolate lab to come in and sniff the parrot. He gives a big sniff and shakes his head. The vet sighs, and repeats his verdict. "The parrot has passed. I wish I were wrong. I'll print up a bill for the visit."

He hands the woman a printed page. "$120! Just to tell me my bird was dead?!"

"Well," says the vet, "You did request the cat scan and a lab report . . ."

How to Take Pictures Like Dad

 Timing is everything when it comes to taking good photos.

Dad always seemed to have an uncanny knack for capturing your best (and worst) moments. But it isn't all Dad mojo or luck. An educated eye for composition, familiarity with good equipment, and practice, practice, practice can make all the difference between passable photos and great ones.

DAD SAYS: "Say Cheese!"

1. No matter what the occasion or setting, try for a mixture of candid shots, planned portraits, and long scenic shots. But unless you're a professional-caliber photographer, focus primarily on the people in your party rather than on the landscape.

2. Use appropriate film: 100- or 200-speed film is great for shooting outdoors or indoors with bright lights or a flash, but it's also fun to experiment with slower film (64-speed) when taking scenic or landscape pictures or high-speed film (400 or higher) when you're taking action or nighttime shots.

3. Even when you're on a hike, do not take pictures of people walking. There isn't a single frame of the human stride that doesn't look awkward when it's frozen in time. The same goes for people eating. No one looks good with their mouth agape!

4. If your subject is particularly shy, take a few steps back, and move around outside her peripheral vision. Use a zoom lens (90 mm) or the zoom function on your digital camera.

5. Think about composition. Try placing your subject slightly off-center in the frame, and use bright flowers, reflections, or colored objects in the fore- or background to balance the shot.

6. Tilt your horizontal axis. Feel free to rotate your camera as you shoot to produce "out-of-the-box" photos. Without the horizon as a constant, clear referent, the figures or objects in the frame will look even more vital and dynamic.

7. When you're shooting landscapes or skyscapes, try "bracketing." Override the automatic focus and aperture features on your standard or digital camera (if you're carrying a little point-and-shoot, this trick isn't for you). Instead of taking a single shot of each scene, take three: one at optimal settings, the next at a smaller aperture setting and faster shutter speed, the last at a wider setting and slower speed.

8. If you want to set up your group shot, try to put faces in every quadrant of your viewfinder. Instead of lining your subjects up, which gives you one line of faces (or, at best, several) and a lot of background, stagger your subjects—one or two sitting, someone kneeling, and a couple standing—so that the whole shot is dynamic.

Essentials of Turkey Carving

Presentation is everything.

When your family piles into the car for a trip, Mom points and Dad drives. When your family pulls up to the holiday turkey, Mom points and Dad carves. Sharpen your knife, take your time, and follow these simple instructions. Then enjoy your moment in the spotlight!

DAD SAYS: "Turkey carving is actually a lot easier than it looks."

1. Make sure that your turkey is thoroughly done. Loose meat around the thigh should actually fall off when it's wiggled.

2. Choose a sharp, thin-bladed knife, with or without serrations.

3. Use your knife to separate the loose thighbones from the body, then remove both thighs and drumsticks. Trim the excess skin for an attractive presentation, and place dark meat on a platter.

4. Insert your knife into the turkey's side, and separate each wing from the body. Trim the wings, and add them to the serving platter.

5. Cutting parallel to the rib cage, take half-inch (1.3-cm) slices from the breast to complete your platter.

6. Bask in the compliments, and enjoy your turkey.

CHAPTER 2:
Handyman Dad

Whenever you want to fix something broken (or improve something that isn't), you can always look to Dad for the save. He might not arrive with lights and a siren, but he's sure to have the whole gamut of tools—plus the know-how that comes from years of experience. Here are a few tips for assembling an appropriate tool arsenal and tackling basic household jobs on your own.

The Kitchen Drawer Tool Kit

Happiness is a good basic tool kit.

Wherever you put them—in a garage or in a big kitchen drawer—you need tools. But which tools? The best way to build a tool-and-gadget shopping list and storage system is to assess the needs and limits of your domestic situation and to be honest about your skill and interest levels. The kitchen drawer tool kit contains nothing more than the bare essentials. It's appropriate for totally inexperienced and novice users, and good to keep for basic emergencies. Read on, and decide for yourself which tools are right for you.

DAD SAYS: "Choosing the right tools for the job is half the job."

Screwdriver

The handiest single screwdriver available can accommodate Phillips-head bits (which fit screw tops that look like a plus sign) on one end and flat-head bits (which fit the minus-sign screw tops) on the other.

> **Tip** Most power screwdrivers are around 7 to 9 volts and are excellent for light home projects. They're usually rechargeable and fitted with their own charging cradles. But think before you buy. For the same price, you can get a more powerful and versatile 12-volt drill.

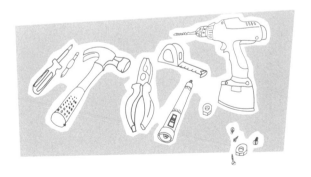

Modest-sized hammer

"Modest-sized" means small enough to fit comfortably in a drawer. Get a claw hammer, rather than a ball-peen—you'll need the claw side for pulling nails and thumbtacks out of walls.

Pliers (standard with cutting edge)

A medium-sized pair of pliers is good for grabbing and twisting anything that your fingers aren't strong enough, small enough, or callused enough to grasp. The cutting edge, located on the back inside of both jaws, is an excellent cutter of wire, fishing line, and plastic price-tag holders.

Needle-nose pliers

Needle-nose pliers are the layman's version of forceps—especially if you have two pairs, one for each hand. They're ideal for fixing jewelry, adjusting wiring, and accomplishing any other task that requires precision in a tiny range of motion.

Utility knife

A good knife features a retractable blade (with a locking mechanism to hold it in place when it's extended) in a sturdy metal body. Spend the extra couple of bucks on a metal knife, and it can serve you well for years.

Tape measure

A garden-variety ten- or 12-foot (3–3.6 m) tape measure is all you need. Make sure that the button for locking the extended metal ribbon in place is operational—you don't want ten feet (3 m) of sharp metal slithering unexpectedly into your face.

Hardware fasteners

Required in every home: nails (large, medium, and small), picture-hanging hooks, screws (both flat and Phillips-head, to fit your screwdrivers), and thumbtacks.

Tape

In addition to Scotch and masking tape (which qualify as household items, rather than shop goods), it's convenient to have a roll of good old silver duct tape at your disposal. Made of water-repellent cloth fibers, it's far more heavy-duty than masking tape. Duct tape can turn a quick fix into a semi-permanent home improvement.

Wall anchors

If you're trying to hang a picture on drywall, these semihollow screws grasp the drywall material once they're in place instead of simply making a hole straight through it. It's always better to put a nail into a wood stud than a screw into drywall (once your wall anchor is in, it can't be removed without making a giant hole), but if your chosen section of wall makes a hollow noise instead of a smart rap when you tap it, you'll need to put down the nail and pick up a wall anchor. Tap the nose into place with a hammer, then use your largest screwdriver to finish the job.

 Tip | One coin-sized magnet will save you hours of labor and—worst-case scenario—a tetanus shot, if you happen to drop your coffee can full of tacks and nails. Instead of fumbling around, simply attract the wayward hardware and convey it back to the can in record time.

Stepladder
If you have to change a light bulb in the overhead or get the turkey platter off the top of the fridge, you'll need a stepladder. The best kind of indoor utility ladder is freestanding and no more than two or three rungs high.

Flashlight
One is good, two are better: keep one in the kitchen drawer and one in your nightstand or under the bed. Check periodically to make sure that the batteries are in working order.

Extension cords and adapters

You'll inevitably need an extension cord to position your appliances exactly where you want them—and always keep an extra for contingencies. If you're living in an older structure without upgraded, grounded outlets (i.e., they'll only accept two-pronged plugs), purchase "cheater" plugs to convert your outlets. The final thing you'll need is a surge protector/power strip, into which you'll plug your computer and anything else you want to protect from sudden cessations and bursts of power.

Small pad of paper

When you make a trip to the hardware store, you'll need to bring a list of your project's specifications—including any measurements or dimensions—plus a list of things to buy. It's best to keep all of this information in the same small note-book, because you'll often need to refer to the information gathered for past projects to complete your present ones. Also keep on hand a pencil, a permanent marker, and a piece of chalk for writing on paper, tape, wall, or any other surface.

Upgrade Kits

The Home Hobbyist Fixer-Upper

The home hobbyist tool kit is one step up from the novice set.
It requires an actual tool box and an efficient organizational
system, plus a broader assortment of superstore esoterica.

Staple gun and staples	Knee pads
Nail guns	Sandpaper with grips
Cordless drill	Angled mirror
High-speed rotary tool	Drywall saw
Level	Clamps
Safety goggles	Allen wrenches
Gloves	

Expert Upgrade Appliances

If you've mastered the techniques for quick fixes, stopgap
measures, and basic improvements, you're ready to graduate
to tougher projects, which will generally require you to cut,
shape, and/or sand your own surfaces. It's time to augment
your gear and graduate to power tools. The expert tool kit
includes powerful, high-torque items that require a workshop
infrastructure for proper storage and operation:

Table with vise	Reciprocating saw
Jigsaw	Compressor
Circular saw	Power sander

Store It All

When you've moved your tools out of the kitchen and into a garage or workroom, you'll need an appropriate place to store them.

In order to keep your tools clean, organized, and ready to hand, install a pegboard wall (like a bulletin board, but with round holes in a regular grid pattern) in your workroom or garage.

1. Hang your tools from hooks set into the holes in an arrangement that puts the tools that you use most frequently in the most convenient placements. Detach electrical cords, and label each one before storing separately; if a cord can't be detached or retracted into the body of your tool, use plastic zip ties to keep it rolled neatly.

2. With a permanent marker, draw an outline around each tool. This outline will tell you where to return each tool after you've used it, and it'll show you which tools have been borrowed by friends or family—or (heaven forbid) stolen.

3. As you modify your tool collection or reorganize it, simply paint over the outlines and start over.

How to Saw Yourself a Hole in One

 When installing components into drywall, it has to look worse before it looks better.

Your walls might look solid, but they aren't. Drywall boards are made of a wood pulp–based composite that's porous (i.e., spongy-looking in cross section) and relatively easy to cut through with your drywall saw. Before you begin any hole cutting to install an outlet, electrical box, or ceiling fan, be sure to put on gloves and a protective mask. Each time you saw through the composite, millions of tiny fibers are released into the air. While these aren't catastrophically harmful to your lungs, they can cause coughing fits and sinus or bronchial infections when aspirated. Don't sacrifice your good health for fashion—wear the mask!

DAD SAYS: "It's all about the stud."

1. Studs are the wooden framing elements of your structure. Whether you're trying to find the most convenient places to hang pictures (at the studs) or to cut holes into walls (away from the studs), you'll need to know exactly where your studs are. Most modern buildings are constructed with studs placed exactly 16 inches (40 cm) apart; it's easy to follow the studs

across a room once you've found the first one. The tried-and-true knock-knock method relies on the idea that your wall sounds less hollow when you hit the stud beneath it. But if you're tired of patching holes caused by mistakes, purchase a stud finder—a small, magnetized block, about the size of a cassette tape, that features a row of lights on one side. When you place the finder on a wall, the magnetic field reacts differently when it encounters wood or metal, and the lights brighten or wink.

2. With a pencil, make marks where the finder shows the most activity or where your knocking indicates studs.

3. Now, determine where and how big you want your hole to be. If you're installing an outlet, an electrical box, or a ceiling fan, hold the unit up to the drywall and trace around it with a pencil. Make sure that your hole will not encounter a wooden stud or any other structural elements.

4. Hold the saw perpendicular to your surface, then use the pointed tip to puncture the upper corner of your outline (use the minimum force required to penetrate the drywall).

5. Drag the saw downward while sawing gently back and forth (as if you were cutting a bagel). To minimize mess, don't remove the saw from the wall until the hole is completely cut. When you come to a corner, withdraw all but the point and twist the handle to change direction.

6. When finished, rub the saw with a damp rag, and leave it to air-dry before putting it away.

How to Patch a Hole in a Jiffy

 Holes happen!

Whether you've put a hole in the wrong place or you encounter a preexisting hole, you'll need to fill it in or cover it up. Small holes require fiberglass tape (mesh covered by clear plastic), a small bucket of drywall compound or mixable drywall powder, a piece of midgrade sandpaper, and a trowel (a flat, flexible piece of metal slotted into a wooden handle).

DAD SAYS: "Plan for the oops: Mistakes are inevitable."

1. Cover the hole with a piece of fiberglass tape. Allow the edges to stick out at least an inch (2.5 cm) on either side of the hole. This will provide support for the drywall compound as you apply it.

2. Open your bucket of drywall compound, and give it a quick stir (make sure it doesn't have lumps); if you're using powdered drywall, follow the instructions for adding water and mixing, then apply the mixture immediately. (It will begin to dry from the moment you add water—within 30 minutes, it will be unusable.)

3. With your trowel, lay a thin coating of drywall over the fiberglass tape (overlap the edges). The first pass should just barely cover your tape. Wait a few minutes to let the patch dry.

4. Sand any rough or heavy spots off your patch. Be careful! If you're too enthusiastic, you'll sand all the way through to the tape.

5. Repeat the troweling/sanding process as necessary, until the outline of your tape disappears and the patch's height and texture are identical to those of the wall.

6. Replace the cover on your drywall bucket so the liquid doesn't dry out; if you've used a powdered mixture, rinse it immediately out of the container you've mixed it in. (Small amounts of drywall, like the residue on your trowel or in your bowl, can be safely washed down your sink. Larger amounts should be chipped off once they're dry then thrown away.)

7. Paint over the white spot. Because drywall is extremely absorbent, you'll need at least two coats. Make the patch as invisible as possible by matching the wall's brushwork and texture.

Big holes—holes that are larger than the diameter of a nail or screw—will require two additions to your shopping list: drywall screws (which have flat heads that won't leave a bump on the wall) and a piece of drywall that's about half an inch (1.3 cm) wider and an inch or two (2.5–5 cm) longer than your hole. Try to get a piece that's approximately the thickness of your wall—and measure *before* you make your trip to the home store.

1. Cut your drywall (with your drywall saw) to the dimensions described above.

2. In the center of the piece, set a drywall screw. Do not tighten this screw all the way down. Leave it sticking out about half an inch (1.3 cm), so you can use it as a handle.

3. Holding the screw, maneuver the drywall through the hole and up behind it, until the front of the patch contacts the back of the wall. Center the patch so the hole is completely covered.

4. Pulling gently on the screw/handle so the patch is held tightly to the back of the wall, put two more drywall screws into the wall—one above and one below the hole—to anchor the patch in place. Now, drive the first screw completely into the patch.

5. Because your wall is probably at least ⅜ inch (1 cm) thick, you'll have to trowel in quite a bit of liquid drywall to bring your patch out to the wall's surface. Once you've reached the surface, follow the steps for patching small holes as described above (without the fiberglass tape) to complete the job.

 Tip If you're patching a hole in the bathroom or an area that gets wet, look for "green board" Sheetrock—it's moisture-resistant and compliant with building codes.

First Aid for a Leaky Faucet

 Know your basic plumbing fixes.

With nothing more than the right equipment and a big dose of confidence, you can tackle many household plumbing problems. Most faucet leaks are caused by rotting or inefficient washers (the discs that fit beneath your faucet's packing nut). To get to the problem, you'll need a wrench (possibly several), rubber gloves (to keep your hands clean and to help you loosen and tighten the assembly without hurting your fingers), and replacement parts as needed.

DAD SAYS: "Don't call in the pros unless you have to!"

1. Turn off the flow of water to the sink by rotating the stop valve on the main pipe, located beneath the sink (generally just before the S-bend). If you can't use your gloved fingers to turn the valve, hit it with your wrench to unstick it.

2. With your fingers, remove the cap from the top of your faucet, and then the handle itself. Use a hex wrench to loosen the packing nut below the handle, and then remove it.

3. Check the washers for wear and tear, and replace them if necessary. (Bring the old ones with you to the hardware store, so there's no room for error when choosing replacement parts.)

4. Make sure that all of the other component pieces fit snugly and that they haven't been roughened or bent over time.

5. To create a tight seal, use waterproof grease on each internal part when putting your faucet back together.

Insulate, Insulate, Insulate!

 Weatherproofing your home is easy and thrifty.

You'd be surprised by how much money you can save on your energy bills by caulking window seams and adding weather-stripping to doors. These tasks require nothing more than some basic materials, a weekend afternoon, and practice with the required tools and techniques. In addition to the financial bonus, you'll be more comfortable. When it comes right down to it, *insulated* is just another word for *cozy*.

DAD SAYS: "Don't turn up the heat—caulk your windows!"

1. Invest in a caulking gun, and choose a caulking material that matches your interior paint color as closely as possible. (Most caulks are not paintable.)

2. Before you squeeze any goo onto your walls, familiarize your-self with the gun's action and the caulk's viscosity by making a few practice lines on newspaper. Squeeze gently on the gun's trigger, and maintain an even pressure as you move the tip along the window seam, applying a thin, even coat of caulk where the window joins the wall. Use a rag to wipe off excess.

3. Caulking does an excellent job of preventing condensation and

eliminating drafts; but if you're still feeling too much airflow, you can apply vinyl or rubber edging to the exterior perimeters of your windows. Like weatherstripping, this edging must be cut to size and purchased at a builder's supply depot (be sure you bring the measurements for each window with you). It slides or snaps onto the window casing much like the rubber wiper blades on your windshield wipers and can be held in place with screws.

 Tip

Old windows may contain glass that is simply too thin to keep the heat in and the cold out. Renters, in particular, are often subjected to this kind of heat loss, because windows (especially old ones) are expensive to replace. Try lining your curtains with a cotton/poly-coated rubberized material (often called "blackout" lining), or cover your windows on the inside with clear plastic sheeting (available at your builder's supply store).

The ABCs of Painting a Room

A fresh coat of paint can take years off a room.

Even if you're repainting in exactly the same color, there's nothing like a new paint job to make you feel as if you've just moved into a brand-new home. Until you've painted, it's hard to believe just how much soot, smog, dirt, and oil can collect on walls and ceilings, making even the most cheerful room look gloomy. But like many other household projects, what appears to be a simple task requires some know-how and the proper equipment. There's always a method to Dad's madness.

DAD SAYS: "When it comes to painting, don't take shortcuts."

1. Measure the room to be painted, then bring the dimensions of your room to the paint store, and consult with an expert to ensure you buy enough paint.

2. Choose your paint color and finish. Unless you're painting a room that gets frequently wet or steamed up, water-based latex paints are generally preferable to the fume-producing, messy oil-based varieties. Flat or semigloss finishes are customary for walls and ceiling, and glossy is the best for trim. If possible, purchase a small test can of your paint color and brush it onto an area of wall that gets a lot of light. Check the color at different times of day to verify that it doesn't turn jaundiced at dusk. If you're using color, think about choosing a contrasting color for baseboards, crown molding, and framing. White trim makes a clean, crisp contrast against virtually any wall color.

3. Purchase several plastic drop cloths (old sheets work just as well), one wide 3-inch (7.6-cm) brush, one narrow 1-inch (2.5-cm) brush, a roller, a roller pan (disposable pans are cheap and convenient), and several roller heads.

4. Remove electrical plates and any stray nails from your walls (fill in large holes as described on page 34).

5. Protect your floors and furniture from accidental splatters. Move objects into the center of the room so they can be easily covered with sheets or a tarp, and use colored painter's tape to cover carpet where it meets the wall or molding. Tape the edges of light fixtures and built-in shelves or cabinets.

> **Tip** Keep a second tarp under you and your ladder at all times, and move it with you around the room—watch out for drips and dribbles!

6. Prepare your wall surfaces. Mix a bucketful of cleaning solution: two parts warm water, one part chlorine bleach or trisodium phosphate. (Make sure you wear gloves and eye protection—especially if you're scrubbing the ceiling. Cover your hair with a scarf to keep it from being bleached by stray drips of cleanser.) Using rags or a large sponge, remove accumulated dirt and oil, especially around light switches or windows. If you or any frequent guests are smokers, give the walls and ceiling a thorough scrubbing. Cigarette smoke leaves a sticky black film.

7. When your surfaces have dried, shake your paint can and open it. Use a flat wooden stirrer to make sure that the paint color and texture are even throughout, and pour a small amount into a paint tray or plastic bowl.

8. With your wide paintbrush, begin "cutting in"—saturating each seam where walls meet or join the ceiling. When you're finished with the ladder work, use the same brush at floor level to coat the bottom of the wall.

9. Use your narrow brush to complete the job by painting into difficult nooks and crannies and around taped obstacles.

10. Next, pour a liberal amount of paint into your tray, and use your roller to coat the large expanses of walls. (And the ceiling, if

you're using the same color for both; otherwise, paint the walls first, and allow them to dry before painting the ceiling.) Rollers will eliminate visible brushstrokes and deposit paint evenly.

11. Let the paint dry completely before applying a second coat.

12. Use your narrow brush and trim paint to coat moldings, base-boards, crown molding, and window frames, and your wide brush to coat your doors. Be careful to keep your brushstrokes uniform and in the same direction (up and down for doors and base-boards, side to side for moldings).

13. When your job is complete, remove your tape from cabinets and carpet, and fold up tarps for reuse. But make sure that the splattered paint on your tarp is dry before you fold it. Thick splatters can remain wet for hours.

How to Unclog a Toilet

 Sometimes jiggling the handle is just not enough.

There's nothing more daunting than a toilet bowl full of refuse that seems to be rising rather than flushing. Keep your bathroom equipped for emergencies, and stay calm throughout the crisis.

DAD SAYS: "It's time to take the plunge."

1. Put on your rubber gloves, take a deep breath, and take hold of your plunger.

2. Hold your plunger perpendicular to the floor, immerse it in the toilet, and place it over the drain opening. Make sure that the entire rubber lip of your plunger is in contact with the porcelain.

3. Take a strong stance, leaning over the bowl to be sure that you're plunging directly downward.

4. Make five or six firm, decisive strokes, and then lift the plunger to see if the change in water pressure has cleared the clog. If the clog is gone, the water will run freely down the drain.

5. Flush the toilet to make sure that the problem is solved.

Tip | If you've repeated the plunging process three or four times without success, try using a plumber's snake (available at most hardware and plumbing supply stores) to snake through the clog, or pour in some drain cleaner to do the job. (Porcelain-safe drain cleaners do work, but they're extremely hard on old pipes. If your bathroom hasn't been remodeled in the last ten years, think twice before opting for the rough stuff.)

Thinking Outside the Fuse Box

 Resetting a circuit is easier than you think.

It seems like no coincidence that "fuse" and "confuse" sound so similar. Where is your fuse box? What does it do? Even if you live in an apartment, it's important to know the answers. Electrical power flows into your house through a main set of wires that run into your fuse box (also known as a circuit breaker). Here, the power is divvied up and sent through separate wires to power outlets and light switches throughout your house.

DAD SAYS: "Practice for emergencies by locating your fuse box in advance."

1. Look for your fuse box to be situated on a wall in the garage, in a closet, in the basement, or near your big appliances.

2. Open the door to your fuse box: inside, you'll find a number of switches that have been labeled by the electrician who installed the box and set up electrical service to your house. Each switch controls the flow of electrical power to a particular room or part of the house.

3. If you're curious, try flipping a switch. Yep, the lights went off. Now, switch it back. Yep, the lights are back on.

4. If too many appliances are drawing power from a single circuit, the circuit can "trip": power will cease to flow to that area of your house. Simply open the fuse box door, and flip the appropriate switch back to the on position.

Picture-Perfect Picture Hanging

A picture is worth a thousand words.

There really is an art to hanging artwork. Novice picture hangers often place their pieces too high—as if they were shelves, rather than eye candy. Think about the last time you walked through an art museum. Did you have to look up at the art? Certainly not! Follow the experts' example, get out your hammer, nails, and stud finder, and set to work.

DAD SAYS: "Keep your pictures at eye level."

1. Follow the methods described on page 32 to find a wall stud so that you can hang your picture securely. You can always use drywall screws if you have to, but it's easier to plan the layout of your "gallery" around the placement of your studs.

2. With a pencil, mark where you plan to place the nail. Remember to factor in the location of the picture's wire or hanger so you can estimate how it will hang on the wall.

3. Lift up your artwork to gauge its weight. Heavy artwork will require a large nail; a framed photo takes a small one. The picture-hanging hardware you choose will be rated for various weights.

4. Using your hammer, pound the picture hanger's nail into the wall, leaving about ¼ inch (.6 cm) protruding. Make sure that you pound the nail at a slightly downward angle so that the picture wire on the back of your artwork will be held securely.

5. Hang your picture. If it's crooked, simply tilt it (incrementally) in the opposite direction until it's sitting straight on the wall. Check your handiwork with your level. Now, stand back and enjoy!

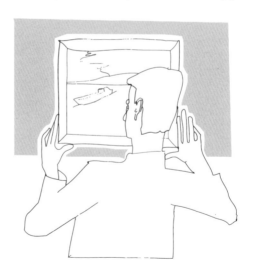

CHAPTER 3:
Dad in the Driver's Seat

Your car is Dad's favorite subject. He's happy to tell you (and tell you again) just exactly how you can find and purchase the perfect car and just exactly how you can keep it running smoothly. The secret is staying in the driver's seat. Don't let a dealer, a "great opportunity," or the mechanical mysteries of your engine drive you to distraction. The more you know, the better equipped you'll be to handle bumps in your road.

How to Smell a Lemon

 When buying a car, make sure you aren't being taken for a ride.

There's nothing like that new car smell . . . it's the most expensive perfume in the world. New cars do offer several advantages: They've never been neglected, abused, or repaired, so you don't have to worry about the vagaries of a checkered past. The down side, of course, is that new cars are expensive. Dad isn't kidding when he says that your car is worth $1000 less from the moment you drive it off the lot.

DAD SAYS: "Don't let a salesperson tell you about the car!"

Arm yourself with information before you visit the lot and take it for a test drive.

1. Know what you want. Determine your specific needs, and you've made a big step toward meeting them. Don't visit a dealership with a vague notion that you need a car and you happen to like a particular manufacturer—you're inviting a salesman to make expensive and potentially irrelevant suggestions. You need to see the car you want, not the car that he or she wants to show you.

Whether you opt for a new car or a used one, shop carefully.

Check the depreciation rates of new cars and the basic Kelly Blue Book values of used cars. The Blue Book, available for sale in bookstores, for reference online, and in your local library, lists the resale value of every car according to its manufacturer, model, and age. If your car is wrecked and your insurance company compensates you for its loss, the insurer will use the Blue Book to determine its worth. When you buy a used car, you will use the Blue Book to look up the car's value and assess the owner's sticker price. And when you're selling a car, you'll use the Blue Book to help determine how much to ask.

2. Prioritize your desires. What's most important to you? Good gas mileage? Styling? Parkability? Price? Weighing these questions will help you narrow your choice down to a particular type of car—say, a subcompact hybrid or a high-performance sedan.

3. Start researching. How many manufacturers make a particular model that suits your needs? Make a list of the contenders, and compare and contrast. Study consumer magazines and online reports to get a feel for how each car stacks up against the others.

4. Now it's time to visit the dealership for a test drive. Call ahead to be sure that the car you want is currently on hand and available for a test drive. When you drive the car, concentrate on how it feels. You'll have plenty of time to fiddle with the stereo and ask esoteric questions, so pay attention to details such as "pickup" (power in acceleration), brake and steering action, and visibility.

Tip **Don't buy the first car you drive! Test-drive the competition so you know what you're missing.**

---

5. Once you've chosen your car, don't fall into financing. Don't sit down to wheel and deal until your salesperson provides you with information on every relevant financing option. Take the brochures home to study them, and don't let the dealer hurry you through the fine print. If you need a loan, shop around to get the lowest interest rate, and make sure you're comfortable

with the specifics of your payment schedule before you sign on the dotted line.

Tip

Clip that coupon! Once you've decided on a car, check your local papers' classifieds. Look for special sales and rebate offers. If you're flexible on color and options, you could pay far less than the sticker price.

---

6. Don't forget to check on the cost of insurance. A new car is nearly always more expensive to insure than a used one, because it has to be insured for the full, undepreciated value.

7. Decide how much you are willing to pay for this car, and get up and walk away if the final figure exceeds it by more than a narrow margin. Know your limit!

8. Once you've purchased your new car, collect the

names (and extension numbers) of your dealer's salesperson, sales manager, finance officer, and service manager. Store one copy of this list in your glove compartment and another in your maintenance file at home. When you have car-related trouble of any kind, it will help you reach the appropriate person immediately.

How to Smell a Used Lemon

 When buying a used car, use the Internet.

Classified ads were once the best places to sell and shop for a used car, but times are changing. The Internet enables car sellers to post more information about their vehicles—including photos—and it lets buyers check the complete (documented) history of any car they please.

Even if you're thinking about buying a car from a friend, jot down its VIN (Vehicle Identification Number) and run it through an Internet background check. There isn't any good reason *not* to do so—even if your friend says the car is perfect.

DAD SAYS: "Never buy a used car from a dealer."

Prices are inflated by the dealer's markup, even though the vehicle isn't new. And the "guarantees" just aren't worth it.

1. Check its teeth. Once you've discovered a good prospect and vetted its history online, contact the owner and meet the car. Go for a test drive, and see how it feels.

2. Have it checked over by a certified mechanic. If you don't already know one (and can't get a good recommendation from a friend), make phone calls to a few local companies and compare prices. Diagnostic services are generally free from your regular mechanic, or between $75 and $100 (price depends on hourly rates) for walk-in customers. Give your mechanic any pertinent information that you've turned up on past failures and repairs, so he or she can check those systems exhaustively.

3. When the job is completed, your mechanic should give you a checklist or computer printout that reports the condition of the mechanical, electrical, and safety systems. If something seems fishy, get a second opinion, but never disregard an expert's research in favor of your own intuition.

> *Tip*
>
> **It might be beautiful, or cheap, or both—but if a car has a history of problems, it's likely to have a future full of problems, too.**

4. Find the Kelly Blue Book value on the car in question, and use that number for a baseline estimate. Now, consider road wear, high mileage, history (including accidents), and environment. If a

car has been driven in snowy areas for most of its lifetime (salt over snow can cause body rust), for instance, it will age faster. All of these factors will reduce the price of a car.

5. Prepare to bargain. Once you've determined the car's net worth, compare it to the seller's price. If your number is lower, just tell the owner how much you want to pay. Justify the difference if there's a big gap. Many owners will rethink the value of their cars when you show them documentation.

6. If the seller still won't budge, walk away. Not negotiating the price generally means that (a) the seller doesn't know enough about the car to know why you're right, or (b) he knows darn

well that there's something wrong with the car, and he's holding out for an ignorant buyer. Find an honest owner, and you'll find an honest car.

7. If you buy the car, do your best to acquire the maintenance file from its former owner—or start a new file. Keep records and receipts from every service transaction so you can easily check your dates and follow a regular maintenance regime.

Car Maintenance Is Next to Godliness

 Routine maintenance uncovers problems before they happen.

There's a lot going on under the hood of your car: Spark plugs are firing, pistons are moving up and down, and belts are going around and around in about ten different places at breakneck speeds. All of this movement can cause damage to crucial parts of your engine, and if you don't keep up to date with routine checks and maintenance, your negligence can have catastrophic results. In addition to following Dad's advice below, read your car manual to make sure that your particular make and model does not require special servicing as well as to find out the recommendations for routine maintenance.

Unless you're an automotive hobbyist—and prepared to cart all waste fluids, chemicals, and parts to the proper facility for disposal—it's generally best to have procedures completed by a mechanic or an auto care franchise. Checking your fluids is one thing, but changing them is quite another.

DAD SAYS: "There's no such thing as benign neglect."

1. Change your oil every 3,000 miles (4,800 km).

2. Change your transmission fluids every 10,000 to 15,000 miles (16,000–24,000 km). Failure to pay attention to your records—not to mention the warning lights on your dashboard—will result in the failure of your engine when it "drops" (i.e., the engine block cracks) due to lack of lubrication. Once this happens, you have to purchase a new engine or fix the old one, which costs nearly as much.

3. Replace your brake pads as they wear out. When brakes start to feel mushy or slow, replace them. Keep driving on worn-out brake pads, and you'll end up needing to replace the entire shoe or drum array—which can cost anywhere from $350 to $500.

4. Rotate your tires and check your alignment every 10,000 miles (16,000 km) or so. Front tires generally show more wear than back tires. Check the outside treads: If they're extremely worn down, you might want to buy a set of new tires. Aligning your

tires properly increases their life span by reducing wear on the inside and outside treads.

5. Get a tune-up whether you think your car needs one or not. Most manufacturers recommend a tune-up at the 50,000-mile (80,000-km) mark, and every 20,000 miles (32,000 km) subsequently, but check your manual—some cars need to be tuned up more often than others. A mechanic will check and adjust the timing of your spark plugs and associated systems to ensure that your car is running at peak efficiency.

Tip | Never leave your car at a garage that won't give you a written statement detailing the repairs, along with a written statement of warranty terms. High-end garages generally offer six-month warranties on repairs, but a 90-day (or even 60-day) warranty is perfectly acceptable, as long as you're getting a good price for reliable service. Be wary of garages that only offer 30-day terms, and never contract to have your car repaired without a warranty (unless your car is a vintage model, which most nonspecialist mechanics will service only on a "hope for the best" basis).

Be Prepared!

Don't try to squash the kitchen sink into your glove compartment, but keep a few basic items on hand.

Keep in the glove compartment:

- Proof of current vehicle registration
- Proof of current vehicle insurance
- Manufacturer's guide to your car
- Detailed city road map
- Pocket flashlight
- Small notebook containing important phone numbers (dealer, mechanic, insurance broker, local police station) and blank pages for notes
- Compact disposable camera (for recording damage and details of accident sites)
- Tissues/napkins
- Emergency sunglasses

Keep in your trunk:

- Jack
- Spare tire
- Emergency tool kit (including lug wrench)
- Towel or sheet
- Rubber or latex gloves
- Yellow pages
- Jumper cables

Do-It-Yourself Fixes: Time for an Oil Change?

 Keep your car running with some easy DIY.

You don't need to go running to a mechanic every time something goes wrong with your car—and in emergency situations, that's not even an option. Purchase a detailed manual for your particular car at any good auto parts store, and keep it in your car. You'll be surprised by the number of things you can fix by yourself.

DAD SAYS: "Put yourself in the driver's seat when it comes to maintaining your car."

1. Check the oil. You don't need to seek professional help to check and top off your oil. Open the hood of your car and look for a small, round handle sticking perpendicularly up from the engine (it looks something like the pull tab on a soda can). Make sure that your engine has been off for at least 15 minutes. (If you pull the dipstick out when the car is hot, the oil will be viscous and partially sucked into the engine block. Thus, the reading will be low.) Simply wipe off the dipstick with a clean rag, reinsert it into the tube, and immediately remove it. Note whether the oil line is at the "full" mark or below the "add" or "low" mark. Consult your car manual to determine the type of oil the engine

requires, and purchase it at your local gas station or auto parts store. Use a funnel to pour it (slowly!) into the reservoir, without overdoing it. Reinsert the dipstick to check the level periodically as you go; do not over fill.

Tip | A surfeit of oil increases pressure inside the engine block, which can cause pressure-related stresses. Lack of oil prevents proper lubrication, creating friction. Metal things moving up and down at extremely fast speeds cannot tolerate friction without sloughing off tiny metal fragments, which can cause your engine to fail or to seize.

2. Check your transmission fluid. If your car seems to shake when you hit the accelerator or if it suddenly lacks power running up hills, it's time to check your transmission fluid. Unlike oil, transmission fluid should be checked when the car is warm (while it's running and just after it's been driven). Look for the transmission fluid dipstick (it should be clearly marked). Just grasp the handle, pull out the stick, clean it with a rag, reinsert it, and quickly remove it. The fluid reading should be at the "full" mark. If the reading is below the "add" mark, you'll need to add more fluid. Purchase the proper fluid for your car from your auto parts store. Add the fluid a little at a time (using a funnel), then start your engine and recheck the levels. Never fill above the "full" line!

3. Check the coolant whenever you check the oil (the car should be cold); make sure to check it before road trips and at least once every six months. Coolant absorbs heat from the engine and moves it to the radiator (just behind the grille) via the water pump, so the reservoir is usually near the front of the assembly. If the level of coolant in the reservoir is below the line marked "low," fill it up. Check your manual to determine what kind of coolant your car requires. *Don't* pour it straight into the reservoir; most cars require you to mix the coolant with an equal proportion of water. Look for instructions in the manual, or ask your mechanic to teach you how.

4. Fix burnt-out headlights. Cars produced before the year 2000 tend to feature easy-access headlights. With a screwdriver, simply remove the plastic headlight cover and remove the bulb. Bring the old bulb to your auto supply store to make sure you purchase the right replacement. Insert the fresh bulb, and then replace the outer

structure without breaking a sweat. Newer cars, unfortunately, make it impossible to change a headlight yourself. You'll need to drive it to your dealer or to a mechanic.

5. Change your windshield wiper blades. Depending on weather and parking conditions, you'll have to change your wiper blades once every two or three years. Whenever your wipers start to streak or smear the water instead of wiping it away, take a look at the rubber squeegee parts of the wiper blades. They might be covered in crud or sap from parking under a tree (in which case you can use soapy water or glass cleaner on a paper towel to fix the problem) or beginning to degrade. If the rubber is granular, cracked, or flaky, it's time for new blades. Simply pop the wiper blades off and take them with you to the auto parts store to purchase appropriate replacements. Then just pop the new ones into place.

6. Change your windshield cleaning fluid. You can purchase a bottle of fluid at any auto parts store and most gas stations, or mix it yourself by combining water and glass cleaner in equal proportions. Simply lift the hood and locate the empty plastic compartment (generally, it's right at the top of the assembly). Unscrew or unsnap the lid, and pour in the fluid.

The Art of Tire Maintenance and Repair

Changing a tire is one skill everyone needs to have.

If you get a flat on the road, you'll need a jack (a pump-handle hydraulic jack works best), a lug wrench, a spare tire, wheel chocks, flares, and a safe place to work. Try to move your car to level ground and as far away from oncoming traffic as possible. To alert other motorists, place three flares behind your car. Distribute them approximately 20 feet (6 m) apart, beginning directly behind your car and working backward. Follow the instructions printed on the wrapper of your flares to light them.

DAD SAYS: "Always carry a spare."

1. Remove your spare tire from the trunk. You should check your spare's air pressure fairly regularly (once or twice a year) with a tire gauge, which will tell you whether it's properly filled. If your spare tire is smaller than the other tires, it's a "donut," or temporary spare. It'll drive you as far as the nearest tire store to purchase a new tire, but it can't make major journeys.

2. Place chock wedges, rocks, or fallen branches in front of your three healthy tires to prevent the car from rolling.

3. Remove the hubcap (if applicable).

4. Using the lug wrench, loosen (but do not remove) the lug nuts.

5. Position the jack under the steel frame or the axle.

6. Now, crank the jack like a corkscrew or pump it with your foot (depending on which kind of jack you've got) to lift your car up high enough for the wheel to come off the ground.

7. Using the lug wrench, loosen the lug nuts on your wheel fully to release the tire. (Be sure to put your lug nuts in a safe place!) Pull the tire toward you.

8. Remove the damaged tire, and store it in your trunk so you can repair it (if it's reparable) or properly dispose it.

9. Place the spare on your wheel rim, and tighten the lug nuts to hold the tire in place. Do not fully tighten the lug nuts at this time.

10. Lower the car by loosening the central nut on your jack.

11. Tighten each of the lug nuts securely.

12. Replace the jack (along with your lug wrench and chocks) in your trunk, and you're on your way.

At the Car Wash

 Take pride in your car, and it will reflect back on you!

You'll extend the life span of your paint job by washing your car once or twice every month. Commercial car washes are fast, easy, and relatively inexpensive. But if you choose to wash it yourself—and doesn't your car deserve your extra TLC?—make sure that you have plenty of soft rags (or several pieces of leather chamois) at your disposal.

DAD SAYS: "A clean car means a happy driver."

1. Fill a bucket with warm water and a few judicious squirts of dish soap, and drag out the garden hose.

2. Wet your car completely with the hose. Then, working from the top down, use a soapy rag to scrub gently over every surface. Soap up the extra-dirty spots, and leave them to soak for a while if they don't come clean right away; do *not* use abrasive pads or cleansers to remove them.

3. Take special care around wipers, mirrors, tire rims, and any other bits of metal or chrome. Stubborn grit should be rubbed off by fingertips cushioned with a soft cloth.

4. When you're finished soaping, use a high-pressure setting on your hose to rinse off the dirty suds.

5. Do not let your car air-dry! Dry windshields and windows first with a clean rag or chamois to reduce streaking and spotting; then move on to drying chrome and metal surfaces.

Wax It!

Wax your car once or twice a year to keep its color strong, shiny, and unrusted—especially if you don't park your car in a garage. Sun, wind, and fog can fade and pit the surface of your car—and eventually, they can cause expensive rust damage to the body. (Coastal conditions are most destructive, because the moisture tends to be salty.)

- Choose a day when the car has just been washed, when you have enough time to finish waxing the whole car in one sitting.

- Read the printed instructions on your car wax before applying it (each brand is slightly different). Generally, you'll use a soft rag in a circular motion to rub it into the paint, and then follow up with another rag to buff up the finish and remove the excess wax.

- Don't wax too often! Wax buildup creates a dull, lifeless finish.

Yessir, Mr. Officer!

When you're stopped by the local police, highway patrol, or any other branch of law enforcement, be nice—even if (and especially if) you don't know why you've been pulled over.

1. Exercise caution when the officer initiates contact. Don't try to ingratiate yourself by getting out of the car before asked to; your movements could be interpreted as threatening. Instead, stay in the car until the officer arrives at your door, and ask to see his or her badge before you roll down the window.

2. The cop should tell you immediately what you've done wrong. If you don't agree with the assessment, don't get angry and defensive. State your case clearly, without any whining or wheedling. The officer can choose to let you off with a warning or ticket you for the infraction.

3. Most tickets (let's face it) are legitimate, even if the law that you've broken seems ridiculous. But if you feel you need to contest the ticket, don't argue on the scene—simply appear for your court date, and let the judge decide.

Always Drive Defensively

 The best driving offense is a good driving defense.

You might be an excellent driver, but other drivers definitely aren't. Accidents occur every day, but if you follow these tips you can be sure that they don't happen to you.

DAD SAYS: "Don't go looking for trouble."

1. Stay out of blind spots. You know where your own blind spots are: on the right and left sides of your car, right behind your bumper— exactly where your rearview mirrors can't see. So driving in someone else's blind spot is like playing chicken: You never know whether they'll look behind them before they change lanes.

2. Don't slide through a red light. Even if you don't get broadsided by an oncoming car, that red light can prove to be expensive. Many cities have installed cameras at major intersections that record your license plate number and enable police to cite you.

3. Don't hurry. Speeding and weaving in and out of lanes might shave some minutes off your travel time, but it increases your chances of meeting with disaster—or with another bad driver. Remember: If you rear-end someone, you are almost *always* at fault.

4. Don't chat on your cell phone. If you have to make or receive a phone call, do it quickly and hang up. A hands-free setup only frees up your hands; it doesn't free up your attention.

5. If you can't see, pull over. If your windshield is dirty enough to cause distortion in heavy sunlight, clean the outside with your wipers, and use a tissue to scrub the inside of the glass. Be sure to put on your sunglasses when you're driving straight into the setting sun.

6. If you get into an accident, stay in control. Don't let angry or hysterical drivers push you around in order to avoid accountability. A quick call to the local police is the best way to avoid disputes and prevent fraudulent claims filed against you. Meanwhile, note down the other driver's name, address, phone number, license plate number, and insurance information—along with the date, time, and location of the accident. Be sure to give the other driver your insurance information as well. Look for witnesses, and take down their contact information.

Parallel Parking Perfected

 Practice makes parallel parking perfect.

Parallel parking is the black diamond of driver's ed (not to mention your driver's test); licenses and healthy egos are won and lost in the completion of this feat. With good parallel-parking skills, you can park virtually everywhere that your car can legally fit—while bad parkers must keep driving round and round the block until they find an easier space. Practice parallel parking on both sides of the street.

DAD SAYS: "Don't pay the high price of a parking garage if you don't have to."

1. Start by signaling your intention to pull into the right or left.

2. Pull up next to the parked car that you're going to be sliding in behind. Your cars should be about even and around 2 feet (60 cm) apart.

3. Check traffic, including your blind spot.

4. Look over your right or left shoulder (right for a right-hand parking spot, left for a left), turn the wheel sharply toward the curb, and reverse slowly. You should be aiming your car toward the far rear corner of the parking spot.

5. Don't wait until your rear wheel hits the curb before straightening out. The moment you begin reversing, begin straightening out with one revolution of the wheel in a smooth, continuous motion. Continue to back in until your front fender clears the rear fender of the car in front of you. This way, you'll glide into your parking spot in a gentle arc, instead of a tight curve.

6. To straighten up, put your car in drive, pull forward (if you need to) to place yourself in the center of the space, and you're done!

Tip   If the space is tight, leave as much room as you can between yourself and the car in front of you to make sure you have room to maneuver when you exit the space.

Taking It on the Road

 Don't just expect the unexpected. Keep chance out of the equation!

Don't wait until the day you leave on a trip to check the road-readiness of your car. Maintenance problems can take several hours—or several days—to fix. If you're using precious vacation time for your journey, those hours and days add up to time you can't afford to lose.

DAD SAYS: "Review your pretrip checklist before you take it on the road."

1. Check the headlights and taillights. You don't want your trip to be spoiled by an encounter with the police and a fix-it ticket. (See how to change your headlight on page 62.)

2. Check the tires. Look carefully at the treads to make sure that they aren't worn enough to inhibit traction. Check the pressure with a tire gauge, and fill them with air at a gas station if necessary.

3. Check your maintenance records to verify that your oil has been recently changed and that you don't need to change the transmission fluid.

4. Check all of your fluids—oil, transmission, and coolant. Add fluid if necessary.

5. Check every visible belt. Cracked belts must be replaced immediately by your mechanic.

6. Check the spare tire to make sure it doesn't need repairs.

7. Wash the windshield, and wipe it down on the inside.

8. Procure a map of your trip and destination city, and mark out your route. Store the map in your glove compartment.

9. Add these items to your trunk: first aid kit, gallon (4 liters) of drinking water, blanket, flares, sneakers and work pants, lantern/flashlight.

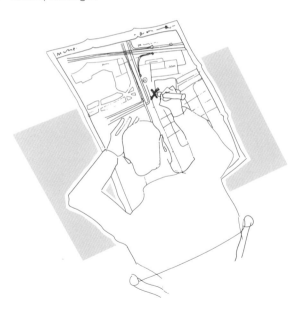

CHAPTER 4:
Dad in the Great Outdoors

Had enough of working around the house? For a change of pace, put the house on your back, pack up the car, and follow Dad into the sunset. Communing with nature, whether you're camping, hiking, fishing, or doing all three at once, is the ultimate way to relax. Do some research and a little comparative shopping, and you can enjoy the outdoors as Dad does, with all of the comforts and safety of home.

Pack Right, Pack Light

 It's all about the bare necessities.

Unless you're planning to hunker down in the snow for a while, your camper's shopping list should be geared toward convenience rather than survival.

DAD SAYS: "Plan ahead, and take only what's necessary."

1. Consider the location and climate (check the weather report) of your campsite, as well as the duration of your stay, and factor in some simple safety features and conveniences accordingly.

2. Whenever possible, contact the campground or study its Web site to apprise yourself of any specific warnings or recent happenings (such as a sudden influx of bears, raccoons, or hard-to-see poisonous plants). The more you know about your campsite's environs, the better you can pack. Timely information can mean the difference between having enough calamine lotion and three days of agonizing itch.

3. Never assume. Determine whether you need a permit or a reservation *before* you set out—don't wait until you get there to find out that you have to turn right around and go home. Contact your national park or nature preserve to acquire any necessary camping permits.

4. Peruse Dad's list of suggested equipment on the following page, and decide which items will best suit your needs.

Tip   Always let a neighbor or a friend know where you're going and when you're expected to be back. Note the campsite's name, phone number, and Web address, plus any other pertinent emergency information. When you arrive at your campsite, check to see if you have cellular service. You might be surprised to find that help is still just a phone call away.

Gearing Up

Most camping gear can be purchased at a one-stop-shop camping/outdoor sporting goods store:

Tent
Camping lantern
Flashlights and
    extra batteries
Camping stove and fuel
Pocket knife
Air mattress
Sleeping bag
Ice/foodstuffs
Water
Iodine tablets/nontoxic
    cleansers
Camping pots/pans
Cooking grate
Hot mitts
Camping dishes/utensils
Fire-starting kit

First-aid kit
Hammer, awl, screwdriver
Bungee cord, laundry line
Duct tape, twine
Cloth gloves, latex gloves,
    cotton gloves
Bug spray
Groceries/sundries
Outdoor clothing
Extra socks (three pairs)
Proper shoes (include one
    pair of flip-flops or
    foam-soled sandals)
Backpack
Fanny pack
Compass
Camera

Your three most important purchases to ensure comfort in the great outdoors? Your tent, sleeping pad, and sleeping bag.

1. Before you buy a tent, determine how many people are going to be staying in it and how cold the weather is going to be. Be realistic: Unless you're planning a winter trip (or a trip into rain and extreme temperatures), go with a car-camping tent or at most a three-season tent. Try out all of the appropriate sizes and models at your local sporting goods and getaway stores. Crawl in, turn around a few times, and lie down. Headroom comes at a price: Taller tents have more wind resistance, which means that they're more unstable (not to mention noisier). Make sure you can sit upright.

   Inexperienced campers should look for a tent that's not only comfortable but also simple to pitch and pack up. If possible, parts and support poles should be interchangeable. Once you've purchased your tent, put it up and take it down once or twice at home. This way, you'll know what to expect.

> *Tip* | Buy an extra set of high-grade stakes. Inexpensive tents often come with spikes that bend when they hit a rock or prove unable to penetrate hard-packed terrain.

2. Sleeping pads offer all the comforts of home in a relatively small package. Air mattresses, foam pads (inexpensive but not very soft), and self-inflating pads (your best choice for a good, warm night of sleep) are available at virtually any camping or sporting goods store. Dad won't leave home without 'em.

3. If you've ever shopped for a comforter, the same rules apply for your sleeping bag: goose down is warmer but more expensive, and synthetic materials are inexpensive but little more than adequate. Keep in mind, however, that your sleeping bag is probably going to get wet. If you opt for a down bag, make sure that you fluff it frequently whenever it gets wet. Feathers are easily crushed, and they tend to get (and stay) clumpy if the bag is rolled up and stored while it's damp. This will drastically reduce your bag's ability to retain heat, so take good care of it.

Choosing a Campsite

 Don't leave the beaten path!

Once you've parked the car, don't head off willy-nilly with your backpack and your tent. Read and obey the signs posted at your campground (or in the informational pamphlet you might have received on your way in) about off-limit areas and potential bear activity. Ideally, your campsite should be big enough to allow you to eat and cook in one area and to sleep in another, with natural barriers (such as trees or a big boulder) or your car in between.

DAD SAYS: "Assess the lay of the land."

1. Tamping down rough ground and grading it for your tent is onerous and dreadfully unfun, as well as hard on the landscape. Try to balance privacy with efficiency by setting up in a flat, well-used site that's out of sight and earshot of other campers.

2. Toilets can be found at most designated campgrounds—make a point of locating them before you settle down. Orient yourself close enough to the latrines to be convenient but far enough away to forget they're there until you need them.

3. Most campgrounds and established campsites are situated for good drainage, out of the path of flash floods, but never forget that the weather can change in an instant. Try not to camp directly beneath large, dry tree limbs. If lightning strikes the tree, you don't want to be crushed beneath falling branches.

4. If you're forced to camp on a slope, make sure that you sleep with your head higher than your feet. Otherwise, your legs will fall asleep and feel miserable in the morning.

Dad in the Great Outdoors

Make Your Own Latrine

Bears poop in the woods, and so can you—especially if the latrines are inaccessible or unusable. Just follow proper protocol:

1. Choose a place at least 200 feet (60 m) away from natural waterways and off the beaten path.

2. Dig a small hole, and commence your business.

3. Try using a handful of grass or leaves for toilet paper (but do so with care; see plants to avoid on page 104); otherwise, seal dirty toilet paper into a ziplock bag so you can pack it out when you leave the campsite.

4. Refill the hole with dirt.

Navigating by Nature

Look to the stars to help you find your way.

Far from home? If you've strayed too far from your campsite in your search for privacy, don't panic. Whether you're stranded during the day or at night, you can orient yourself by nature's landmarks: a specific tree or rock formation that you remember as a signpost, the directional growth patterns of tree branches and moss, or the positions of constellations.

DAD SAYS: "Keep calm, and remember Dad's basic navigational survival tricks."

- When you first set out on a hike, take careful mental notes of the natural formations all around you. Look for dead trees or other natural landmarks that can point you in the right direction when you retrace your steps.

- You can also orient yourself by the sun as you walk. Given the general time of day, note the direction that your shadow is pointing. For example, you might walk toward your shadow "head" on the way out, and away from it when you retrace your path.

- On a cloudy day, check the growth patterns of tree branches and of moss on tree trunks. In the Northern Hemisphere, horizontal tree branches (and mosses) grow in greater abundance from the southern sides of tree trunks. In the Southern Hemisphere, the reverse is true.

- At nighttime, you can navigate by the stars. First, find the Big Dipper—which, true to its name, looks exactly like a giant soup ladle. During spring and summer in the Northern Hemisphere, the Big Dipper (or Ursa Major) is high in the sky from evening onward and bright enough to be visible in major urban areas.

Dad in the Great Outdoors

Focus on the two stars that form the end of the Dipper's bowl. These two stars point directly at the North Star, which is a bright star of the same intensity as the ones that make up the Big Dipper. Once you've found the North Star, you've determined the direction of true north from your position. (The North Star is also the end of the handle of the Little Dipper. Look carefully, and you'll find a smaller ladle that's curved in the opposite direction from the Big Dipper.)

Your Quest for Fire

 Don't forget your fire-starting kit.

Without a little fire, camping can be a miserably cold and dangerous pursuit—so always pack several fire-starting aids. Never assume that someone else is going to bring the water-proof matches or the cigarette lighter, even if they volunteer to do so. The words "You said *you* would bring them" won't make you any warmer on a drizzly, cold night in the woods.

DAD SAYS: "Always bring a backup for your backup!"

1. Bring the right fire-starting gear. Cigarette lighters are easy and safe, but they're also unreliable. Back them up with waterproof matches or matches kept dry in a ziplock bag.

2. Make sure you have a reliable source for firewood. If you know that you won't be camping in a location where coals in a fire pit are allowed, bring your own firewood—especially if you're going to a high-traffic campsite where fallen branches are scarce. To supplement your wood, look for deadwood or driftwood on river-banks. (*Never* cut down trees.)

3. Find a good place for your fire pit. If possible, find a flat area about 20 feet (6 m) in diameter that's bordered on one side by boulders

or trees. Make sure that there is at least 10 feet (3 m) between your prospective fire pit and any trees, bushes, and undergrowth. There should also be at least 10 feet (3 m) between the fire pit and your tent and car.

4. Designate your fire pit. If a ring or cairn of rocks hasn't already been built, this is a good indication (along with all of the posted signs) that coal fires aren't welcome. Don't build a pit that will intrude upon nature. Simply clear the space and tamp it down to prevent dust and chaff from sparking and blowing around in the breeze.

5. Assemble and light your fire. If you're building a wood fire, assemble a pile (about the size of a flattened football) of kindling. Dry leaves, grass, and other dead plant material work best (if you need to, you can augment it with newspaper). Make your pile loose, so that oxygen can circulate. Then surround it with a tepee of twigs: Stand the twigs on their ends and lean them together over the kindling. Light your kindling with a waterproof match or lighter. For a coal fire, heap your coals in the center of the fire pit, and

soak them in lighter fluid, then use an extra-long match or
lighter to ignite the fire.

6. Feed your fire. If you've made a wood fire, add one or two pieces
of collected or packed-in firewood at a time.

 **Don't make a hot, fast-burning fire. Keep it modest and
contained, and stay aware of changing wind conditions,
dryness, and extreme heat.**

Camp Cooking Gear Basics

 The only thing better than home-cooked is
camp-cooked.

The best thing about food cooked in the wilderness is that no
matter how bad it actually is, it always seems to taste great!
Still, it's a good idea to shoot higher than franks 'n' beans—you
might surprise yourself, if you bring the right ingredients and
the right equipment. Camping stores offer neat sets of nestable
pots and pans, with removable handles that can be tucked
inside the stack. But however nifty they seem, don't purchase
any items that don't look durable enough to withstand the high
heat of your cookfire or camp stove.

DAD SAYS: "Don't forget to kiss the cook."

1. Take one large stockpot, one small- to medium-size saucepot, and two skillets—one large and one small. Nonstick finishes are great when it comes to washing up, but they tend to get scraped and flaky from rough treatment. If you do go nonstick, don't forget your plastic spatula.

2. Bring one large bowl for marinating meat, scrambling eggs, or stirring pancake mix.

3. Bring two large, stackable heavy-duty basins in which you can wash dishes—one for soaping (with nontoxic, environment-friendly soap) and one for rinsing. Metal dish basins can be filled with water and heated directly over the fire or on the stove while you're eating, but watch your fingers when you wash; you don't want to burn yourself on the hot sides or bottom. Thick plastic basins are lighter to pack and more flexible, but you obviously can't put them directly on the stove. You'll have to heat the water in an unused pot and pour it in.

4. Bring long forks or skewers for roasting marshmallows and hot dogs—don't count on finding a perfect stick in the wild.

5. Bring a plate, bowl, and mug for each person on the excursion—plus one extra of everything. Dishes should be nonbreakable (metal or heavy plastic is best) and easy to stack and pack.

Doing Dishes in the Wild

It's wonderful to keep your dishes (and yourself) thoroughly clean while you're camping, but don't sacrifice the ecosystem in the process.

- Use small amounts of nontoxic, eco-friendly cleansers, and do not empty soapy water into natural ponds or streams.

- Strain large bits of food out of rinse water with your strainer, seal them in a plastic bag, and pack them out with you.

- If you're making a day or weekend trip, haul your dishwater at least 200 feet (60 m) from natural water sources, and disperse it over a wide area of bare ground or undergrowth.

- If you're going to be camped in one place for more than two days, dig a sump: a deep, narrow hole (about 3 feet [.9 m] deep and 1 foot [30 cm] in diameter), at least 200 feet (60 m) from natural water sources, into which you can safely pour your strained dishwater. Just refill it with dirt when you leave.

- Use good camping etiquette whenever you're tending to personal business, and especially when you leave the campground. Spit toothpaste into the sump or the fire pit.

6. Don't forget silverware: one set (including steak knife) for each person, plus an extra set.

7. For cooking utensils, bring one spatula (if you're using nonstick pans, make it plastic), one ladle, two large spoons, one strainer, one carving knife, and one serrated knife (for slicing bread).

8. Bring a couple of plastic ice chests: one for food, one for beverages.

9. Purchase ice for both coolers. Store the ice in your coolers in their unopened plastic bags to avoid the formation of a cooler swamp. Melted ice can be used as dishwater or for putting out an evening fire.

10. To leave the wilderness as you found it, pack all human detritus into small plastic bags, and store the bags in the car and away from the campsite for later disposal. That means leftover food, empty cans and bottles, and anything else that can't be safely burned in your fire should be packed away. Ziplock bags are vital when it comes to storing material that you never, ever want to touch again.

Roasting on an Open Fire

 The secret to gourmet food in the great outdoors is variety.

You aren't on rations here—you're having fun! An assortment of basic ingredients designed to satisfy every savory, salty, sweet, juicy, or crunchy craving you might have will add immeasurably to your quality of life. At the same time, be practical. When assembling your camping larder, choose foods that are easy to roast or stew.

DAD SAYS: "Make it as easy as possible to satisfy your hunger or peckishness so you can get back to all of the best parts of your camping experience."

Cut down on your prep and cooking time by doing as much of the grunt work as possible before you even leave the house:

- Prebaked potatoes can be left wrapped in foil in your cooler until you're ready to warm them up in the coals.

- Precooked bacon and brown-and-serve sausage cook quickly in a frying pan, and smoked lunch meats make excellent sandwiches.

- Roastable vegetables can be washed, cut or sliced, and divided into foil packets while you're still in your home kitchen—not only to save on time and labor while you're in the wilderness but to ensure that you have all of the proper seasonings and prep tools at your disposal. Remember: You can't take everything with you.

Pack the following essential ingredients for your weekend camping trip:

- Powdered juice drink (1 can) or iced tea (1 large canister)
- Coffee, ground (1 ziplock bag full)
- Bottled water (1 gallon/3.7 l per person)
- Fruit (4 pieces per person)
- Lunch meats (16 ounces/ .5 kg per person)
- Condiments
- Spices, salt, pepper
- Fresh garlic (4 heads)
- Bread and/or buns (½ loaf or ½ dozen per person)
- Butter (1 stick)
- Milk (1 gallon/3.7 l)
- Eggs (1 dozen)
- Cheese (1 pound/450 g)
- Instant pancake mix (1 large box)
- Maple syrup (1 bottle)
- Instant oatmeal (1 large bag)
- Peanut butter (1 jar)
- Jam (1 jar)
- Hamburger or veggie burger mix (¼ pound/ 113 g per person), hot dogs (2 packages)
- Veggies (roastable pre-made packets) (8 or more)
- Potatoes (2–4 per person)
- Lemon (1)
- Canned stew, soups, beans (4–6 cans)
- Nuts (2 pounds/900 g)
- Flour and/or cornmeal (for frying fish, 1 ziplock bag full)
- High-energy bars/trail mix (1 dozen)
- Nontoxic cleanser (1 bottle)
- Sponges (1 or 2)
- Paper towels, handy wipes (1 roll)
- Large garbage bags (1 for each day)
- Medium ziplock bags (1 box)

Now that you've got your ingredients, how's about a little fire to get them all cooking?

1. First, create your roasting pit. Scoop some of the hottest embers out of the center of your fire, and mound the coals into a pile. Smooth a hollow into the top, and you're ready to start cooking.

2. Wrap each serving—veggie, corn, potato, meat, or a combination of several—in foil. Make sure the foil is completely sealed, so that none of the juices can escape (keep seams on the top of the packet, rather than on the sides).

3. Wrap each packet in several layers of newspaper. Don't wad the paper. Keep your bundles flat. Wrap them in one more layer of foil.

4. Place the packets in the coals, and cover them completely. The heat will penetrate your packets from all directions and cook each item evenly, with no burned bits.

5. Leave packets on the fire for roughly the same amount of time you'd need to bake them in the oven: 15 to 20 minutes for corn and veggies, 45 to 50 minutes for potatoes and meat.

Dad's Twice-Roasted Cheese 'n' Garlic Stuffed Spuds

1. Wipe (or wash) one large spud per person, and wrap each separately in foil. Make a roasting pit (described on page 86; if you've got a wood fire, just use the hottest part of the fire), and bury the spuds. Roast for 30 minutes.

2. While the spuds are roasting, mince two fresh garlic cloves (add more to taste) and grate ¼ pound (113 g) of cheese. Combine cheese, garlic, ½ teaspoon (2.5 ml) of salt, and ½ teaspoon (2.5 ml) of pepper in a bowl.

3. Remove spuds and unwrap. Slice potatoes lengthwise, and use a spoon to hollow out the halves. Add half of the potato to your garlic-cheese mix.

4. Fill the hollows with cheese-garlic-potato mix, put the potato halves back together, and rewrap in foil.

5. Continue baking for 20 minutes. Unwrap and enjoy!

S'more, Please!

There isn't much you can do to improve the taste of Dad's old s'mores.

1. Toast a marshmallow to the perfect mushiness (or burn it, if that's your pleasure).

2. Sandwich the marshmallow with half of a chocolate bar between two graham crackers.

3. Optional: Return the sandwiched s'more to the fire for a perfectly melty mess.

For variations, try using gingersnaps instead of graham crackers—or a crackle bar instead of plain chocolate.

Roas-terrific Nuts!

Chestnuts aren't the only things that taste great when roasted on an open fire. Any largish nuts—pecans, walnuts, pine nuts, and hazelnuts—will do.

1. Simply wrap the nuts (still in their shells) in foil.

2. Bury them in coals (or in the hottest part of your fire).

3. Cooking times depend on the size of the nuts and the heat of your fire. Test-roast a few medium to large nuts for 5 to 10 minutes, and add or subtract time as needed on the next batch.

Coffee Counts

Coffee is just as important to your quality of life in the wilderness as it is in the city. Don't skimp by settling for instant, freeze-dried coffee.

- Stovetop percolators—which you can use just as easily in your kitchen at home—have built-in filters and a foolproof method for delivering excellent coffee (beans should be coarsely ground).

- Stovetop espresso makers take the same principles one step further, by adding another filtering attachment for extremely fine grounds.

- For quick single cups, check specialty or high-end grocery stores for prepackaged single-serving coffee cup/filter arrays. These paper products are easy to burn in your campfire when you're ready to leave, and they'll deliver tasty coffee in minutes—just add one scoop of coffee per cup.

- Your last option is the old "cowboy coffee" method. Simply dump boiling water into your grounds (in a cookpot) and let it simmer for several minutes. Take the pot off the heat to let the grounds settle, then carefully pour it off the top into cups. You'll be straining coffee grounds through your teeth, but if you want to feel the true grit of roughing it, this is a good way to do it.

Critterproof Your Campsite

Don't forget: You're crashing *their* party.

Bears and other wild fuzzies are smart . . . and they know a great opportunity when they see one. After all, if you had to choose between stalking prey and foraging through miles of wilderness or picking through the larder of a few dumb campers, which would you choose? Cut down on temptation. Contain the smells from your cookfire and campsite, and always follow campground regulations regarding lockers and bear boxes.

DAD SAYS: "It's easy to protect your foodstuffs from the depredations of small animals—and even bears."

1. Make sure the lids of your coolers are tightly fastened (wrap your coolers with bungee cord, if you want to be certain), and put anything that smells good—even toothpaste—in your car.

2. Follow your campground's instructions on storing garbage. If it can't be kept in your car (or if you've left your car behind), you'll have to secure a laundry line or sturdy cord to a tree limb, and suspend the bag about 6 to 8 feet (1.8–2.4 m) off the ground (make sure the top of the garbage bag is tightly sealed and that the bag itself is heavy-duty enough to

rebuff sharp beaks and claws). This setup should be at least 20 feet (6 m) upwind of your campfire and your tent.

3. Deterring bears is quite a bit harder. Many campgrounds offer rentable storage lockers—heavy, bearproof boxes—for food and garbage. Situate the box far from your campsite (at least 20 feet [6 m] upwind); fill the box in the evening, and lock it. Place it on even ground so the bear can't roll it away, and far enough from tree trunks that he can't prop it up to try to smash it.

Backcountry Bearproofing

 Remember: Bears are smarter than you think!

Without a bearproof box, it's wise to hang your food from a tree. You'll need two garbage bags, two canvas laundry sacks, about 75 feet (23 m) of laundry line (or heavy cord), and a hammer.

DAD SAYS: "With a little ingenuity, you too can beat the bears."

1. Walk about 50 feet (15 m) from your campsite, and find a tree limb about 12 feet (3.6 m) long and 25 feet (7.6 m) off the ground.

2. Divide your stuff between two garbage bags, close them tightly, and put each bag completely inside a laundry bag. Cinch the necks, and tie the cinching cord in a knot.

3. Cut one 12-inch (30-cm) piece of laundry line, pass it under the cinching cord of one bag, and knot it, leaving a large loop. (This will be your handle, when you return in the morning to claim your bags.)

4. Unwind the rest of your laundry line. Tie one end to the neck of your hammer and the other (very securely) to the neck of a laundry bag.

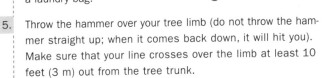

5. Throw the hammer over your tree limb (do not throw the hammer straight up; when it comes back down, it will hit you). Make sure that your line crosses over the limb at least 10 feet (3 m) out from the tree trunk.

6. Using the line as a pulley, hoist the bag. Don't stop pulling until the bag reaches the limb.

7. While keeping the line taut, retrieve your hammer, and untie it. (Step on the line to keep it taut, so you can use both hands.)

8. Pass the end of the line through the cinching cord, and keep pulling it through until the slack is taken up. Lift up the bag as high as you can, and keep pulling the slack.

9. Tie the line securely to the cinching cord, and stuff the slack inside.

10. Lift the bag over your head; the first bag will begin to descend like a counterweight.

11. Use a long stick to poke the second bag higher, until both bags hang at nearly equal levels about 15 to 18 feet (4.5–5.4 m) off the ground.

Sorry, Yogi! You're out of luck.

First Aid Gone Wild

 Safety *always* comes first!

Each time you go camping, assemble a first aid kit that's appropriate for your location, duration of stay, and the specific medical needs of the members of your party. Find out—by researching online or calling the campground—which poisonous animals and insects are likely to be living in or near your campsite, and bring an antivenom kit if necessary.

DAD SAYS: "An ounce of prevention is worth a pound of cure."

- Mosquitoes, sand fleas, and ticks can put a damper on anyone's high spirits. Keep your repellent (in spray or lotion form) where you can easily reach it while you're still in the car. If you don't apply it before you get out and start unpacking, you could be eaten alive before you reach the bag in which you've stored it.

- Zip your tent at night, and keep it zipped during the day. Bug repellent doesn't keep you from being probed and crawled on by the insects that take up residence in your tent.

- When you need to get water from a stream or other possibly contaminated source, be sure to use your iodine tablets/water purification kit. Put one tablet per quart (.9 l) of unpurified water (or two tablets, if the water looks especially dark) in your empty plastic water bottles, allow 30 to 45 minutes for the chemical to kill any microorganisms, and drink up.

- Cold air, high winds, and dust can cause eye irritation and dryness. Use saline drops to moisturize eyes and remove chaff (tiny foreign objects). If you can't see, you can easily fall or twist your ankle by stepping in a hole or on uneven ground.

Don't Forget Your First-Aid Kit

A basic adult first-aid kit should contain the following:

Athletic tape
Adhesive bandages
Ace bandages
Gauze
Moleskin
Mercurochrome/betadine
Antibiotic cream
Steroid cream
  (hydrocortisone)
Calamine lotion
Antihistamine
Pain relievers
Motion sickness relievers
Altitude sickness relievers

Electrolyte powder
  (for hydration)
Antidiarrheals
Antacids
Vitamins
Aloe vera gel/dry skin lotion
Saline solution
Tweezers
Cuticle scissors
Sewing scissors
Needle and thread
Extra lighter
Sunscreen

- Even if you're wearing thick socks, long pants, and hiking boots, ticks can find a way to bite you. Check your legs and arms (and just about everywhere else, even your neck and scalp) when undressing for bed and before dressing in the morning to make sure you haven't picked up a passenger.

- Poison oak, poison ivy, and stinging nettles can ravage skin on contact, causing a painful burning itch that gets worse as you scratch it. Always keep your fingers away from that itch!

Poison ivy and poison oak can spread through touch to other parts of your body—and to other people's bodies, as well.

Tip   Nature's general rule of thumb seems to be that plants that grow with groupings of odd-numbered leaves are bad for you to touch, while plants with even-numbered groups of leaves are safe. If you get it backward (or fall into a patch of poison oak), rub calamine lotion on affected areas to soothe the itch, then put on a pair of cloth gloves to keep yourself from scratching.

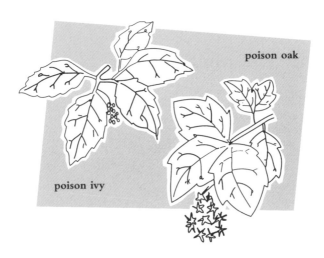

poison oak

poison ivy

Tick Tips

Unlike sand fleas and other biting nasties, ticks are arachnids. In size, their round bodies can range from the diameter of a pinhead to that of a brass tack—i.e., from nearly invisible to nightmarish. As they feed on your blood, they inflate—so the small, hungry ticks that are at first hard to find can become all too easy to see once they're bloated. If you find a tick, don't try to pull it out without the proper equipment. Its head will be completely buried under your skin, and you must encourage the tick to retract its head before removing it. If the head is left inside you, the bite will become painfully infected.

1. Grip the body of the tick with tweezers, as close to the surface of the skin as possible. Gently but firmly, pull backward in one straight, continuous motion; do not wiggle the tweezers from side to side, as this motion can cause the tick's thorax to separate from its head.

2. If this doesn't work, grip the tick with your tweezers (as described above), and heat its abdomen with a lighted match or lighter. Pull until its head pops out.

3. Do not release the tick from your tweezers until you have determined whether the head is attached. If it's all in one piece, throw it into the hottest part of your fire. If you've only got the body, use the tweezers again to attempt to pull out its head or mouth parts. Then use an ink pen to circle the bite and prepare for a trip to the doctor. In addition to bacterial infections, victims of tick bites in certain states can contract Lyme disease—so don't try to grin and bear it. Get it treated.

At the Fishing Hole

Nothing beats fishing for feeling at one with nature.

Where does Dad get all of those Big Fish stories? Find out for yourself by camping in a fishing-friendly location. The caretakers of many popular lakes and ponds don't leave things to chance. They stock the water with fish eggs and/or baby fish and carefully nurture them to adulthood so that you and your dad can have a fun, fulfilling fishing experience. It's not quite like shooting fish in a barrel, but your chances are definitely good.

DAD SAYS: "Never open a can of worms—unless you're planning to go fishing!"

1. Plan ahead. Farmer's almanacs (and many good calendars) will show you a date-sensitive chart of the phases of the moon. This information can be crucial to catching fish that tend to be more active and catchable under certain conditions. For instance, some fish like to feed during a full moon, while others prefer different segments of the lunar cycle. Muddiness, water temperature, and strength of current are changeable and very much dependent on the moon. Take the local experts seriously. If an old salt tells you that it's no use putting a hook in the water until midnight, plan to stay up late.

2. Buy the right pole. For as much as you'd spend on renting decent fishing equipment for the weekend, you can buy a passable pole and accompanying fishing kit (including a tackle box and a sampling of hooks and lures) that contains virtually everything you'll need. Even basic poles come in several sizes designed not only for small, medium, and large people but to catch small, medium, and large fish.

3. Choose the right bait. Stop at the fishing supply shop that's closest to your destination, and ask the proprietor what type of bait you should purchase. Each species of fish is more attracted to certain kinds of bait than to others, but within those general guidelines, there's a lot of room for trial and error. Trout, for instance, respond well to night crawlers—but Dad can no doubt suggest any number of tasty tidbits that have proved to be successful in the past, from hunks of string cheese to live crickets.

Hook 'Em Up!

- When hooking large earthworms like night crawlers, look for a band near the back of the head, and insert your hook just behind it (otherwise, insert the hook approximately half an inch [1.3 cm] away from the worm's head).

- Push the hook through until you have enough room left at the tip to thread it in and out of the worm again, and repeat the process about an eighth of an inch (.3 cm) away from where you made the first insertion. The point is to cover the hook completely, so the fish won't see any metal glinting.

- If you're hooking a cricket, be prepared to lose a few insects before you finally get it right: Grasp the insect firmly between your fingers, and stick the hook into the joint between head and thorax. Then thread it downward into the cricket until it emerges from the middle of the abdomen. This is a simple process, but definitely not recommended for the squeamish.

4. Cast your line. If you're a novice, read the instructions that come with your pole, and watch what Dad and the other pros do. Do not simply fling your bait into the air and hope it comes down in a good spot. Hold the pole perpendicular to the ground (like a flagpole) and flip the bail so the line runs freely. Then flick the rod from perpendicular to parallel in a pointing motion, as if you're aiming a gun.

Got Guts?

You got lucky! Now it's time to get dirty. Before your fish goes into the frying pan, you'll have to clean it.

1. Choose a short, sharp knife, and put on latex gloves.

2. Look for the pectoral fins, which emerge from the ventral (bottom) side of the fish where the tail begins to narrow.

3. Stick the point of the knife between the fins, with the cutting edge pointed toward the head, then slice forward until you reach the gills. Make sure you cut deeply enough to completely open the abdomen.

4. Insert your finger into the top of the incision (at the gills), hook the innards, and pull down and backward, toward the fish's tail. Everything should come sliding out (use your other hand to grab the guts as they emerge).

5. Unless you've caught a catfish or a similarly scaleless fish, you'll have to scale the fish (especially if you plan to cook it in its skin). Using a dull knife, scrape against the nap, or direction of growth, of the scales. It's easiest if you keep the fish in a bucket of water while you scale it.

6. Dispose of your fish guts responsibly. Do not throw them back in the water. You shouldn't contaminate a source of water that might be accessed by campers further downstream or interest the noses of itinerant bears. Dig a hole far from your campsite and bury the guts, or burn them in your fire.

Dad's Simple Pan-Fried Fish

Figure on serving one (or more, if you got lucky) fish per person.

1. On your cooking grate, preheat an oiled frying pan.

2. Lightly coat each fish in cornmeal or flour; add salt and pepper to taste.

3. Cook fish until slightly browned on each side.

4. Serve with lemon.

Row, Row, Row Your Canoe

 Put your paddle to the test.

For a lovely—and fish-free—day on the water, you can always opt for paddling a canoe. Many campgrounds offer rental canoes, paddles, and even canoeing lessons. If you're new to the pursuit, take advantage of as much expert advice as you can. Paddling a canoe might look simple, but it's a devilishly difficult skill to master.

Dad Says: "Hope you like getting wet!"

1. Lower yourself into a kneeling position when you get into the canoe, just behind the middle of the craft.

2. Place one hand on the end of the paddle and the other about 30 inches (76 cm)—or slightly more than one arm's length—further down toward the blade. Keep the blade perpendicular to the water.

3. Without raising your butt from your heels, lean as far forward as you can to dip the blade into the water, then pull back with your bottom hand while pushing with your top hand. Don't let the blade get behind you. You should never pull back farther than your own hip.

4. Lift the blade out, and turn it parallel to the water (to cut down on wind resistance) as you move it back into position for another stroke.

CHAPTER 5:

Dad on the Home Front

Dad's home is his castle. Your house, on the other hand, is four walls and a roof. What makes the difference? Pride, awareness, and a lion-defending-his-den feeling of ownership, even if you're renting. Dad is a benevolent despot, nurturing every aspect of his domain—from his lush front lawn to his uncluttered downspouts. He's famous for his high-watt holiday extravaganzas and envied for his peerless BBQ skills, which he likes to show off as often as he can. If you want to build a castle, try living like Dad. It's hard work, but it's worth it!

Your Home Away from Dad's Home

 Your rental apartment or house should be safe, secure, and a good deal all around.

When you move into any rental house or apartment, Dad never fails to ask questions. Is it clean? Is it safe? How's the neighborhood? Are you getting a good deal?

DAD SAYS: "Don't sign a lease before you know all the answers—and make sure that the landlord knows them, too."

1. If you're looking for a home in a crowded or highly desirable location, allow yourself at least one month to secure a place.

2. Find out how the natives shop for housing. Some cities have online bulletin boards that are successful enough to supplant the newspaper want ads almost completely.

3. Check listings every morning, and call or e-mail the landlords (or management companies) immediately. Most landlords make appointments on a first-called, first-called-back basis.

4. Go early to open houses. Many landlords prefer to meet all of their prospective tenants at once, at two- or three-hour-long open houses. Be there when it starts. Early tenants make a good impression on landlords; they tend to look more responsible and more likely to pay their rent on time.

5. Dress nicely. You don't have to put on a tux, but you should look mature and prosperous, as if you bring home a big, fat, regular check.

6. Bring a filled-out rental application (you can download and print one out online at any site that carries rental listings) and credit report. Even if the landlord requires you to fill out his particular application, attach your copy when you turn it in.

7. Be professional. When you interview with the landlord, keep your cool; be excited about the place, but don't gush. Answer questions concisely, without being (or seeming) evasive, and ask a few questions of your own. Keep it general, especially if you're competing with other prospective tenants.

8. As you walk through the apartment, check the water pressure, any telltale signs of leaks (water-stained ceilings are a sure indicator of water damage), the general state of the walls and flooring, the security system, the smoke detectors, and the condition of all the appliances to be sure that everything is generally clean and in good working order.

9. Read the fine print, and then review the details. Would you be renting the apartment on a month-to-month basis or signing a six-month or year-long lease? Is your rent due on the first or the fifth of each month? Who pays for utilities? Are you allowed to have pets? Do you share a parking space, or do you have your own? What are the clauses regarding subletting and increases in rent?

10. Don't be afraid to negotiate. If the security deposit sounds outrageously high, suggest a new sum. The landlord might be working for a property management company or conglomerate, which sets a nonnegotiable deposit amount, or he might not—in which case, he can work with you.

11. Before signing the lease, do a walk-through of the apartment with the landlord. Inspect every room, and note any observed damage to walls, ceiling, carpet, or flooring, so that your landlord won't charge them to you when you move out. Pay special attention to the condition of the kitchen and bathroom. Be sure you check the plumbing and look inside the oven and the fridge. Make sure that the appliances and all of the power outlets work—just bring an electrical tester (an inexpensive, penlight-like tool that lights up when the tip is inserted into an active outlet), or get an electrician friend to help you.

Renter's and Landlord's Responsibilities

Whenever you sign a rental agreement, you agree to maintain the property in its current condition, as does your landlord. He or she is legally obligated to keep your building (including driveway, walkways, stairs, patio, and deck) safe and in good repair.

- Depending on your local rental and building codes, "good repair" generally means that all appliances must be functional—in many areas, your landlord can't even charge rent for the days that your heater isn't working; that windows can be opened and shut and aren't cracked or broken; that all door locks are solid; and that your address numbers are clearly marked on the building and on your mailbox.

- If your rental unit includes a yard, your landlord is also required to maintain the landscaping and eliminate fire hazards.

- When anything breaks or begins to wear out, call your landlord immediately to request repairs. If he doesn't respond, e-mail or fax him a written request. Some landlords employ building managers or supervisors to oversee upkeep (make sure you ask your landlord about repair protocol when you sign your rental agreement), but *someone* needs to respond to your request. Otherwise, say that you'll fix the problem yourself—and take the service charge out of your rent.

Say Howdy, Neighbor!

 Be a good neighbor.

Your abode isn't an island. Whether it's sparsely or densely populated, you live in a *community*. Get to know the people who work at all of your customary haunts, and call them by name. Keep an eye out for vandals, shoplifters, and any suspicious activity around these businesses, and tip off the proprietors. If you're ever in a pinch or need a special favor from them, you'll be glad you made the effort.

Being friendly will also keep you safer, by netting you a team of neighbors who will be looking out for you. And who knows? You might discover your soul mate or a lifelong friend in this former group of strangers.

DAD SAYS: "Get to know the lay of the land."

1. Take a walk! Even if you don't drive to work—and especially if you do—make a point of strolling around the block once or twice a week. It's a nice way to relax and to notice details in your environs that you'd never otherwise see.

2. Read the local paper. Find out what's going on in your community. In addition to neighborhood stories, you'll get listings of local

events and entertainment options. Keep an eye out, as well, for news on pending road improvements and transit changes.

3. Be a part of the solution. If you really want to get involved, find out if you can join a Neighborhood Watch program or start attending community meetings, where local issues are raised and addressed by residents and officials.

4. Know your neighbors. If you aren't on chatting terms already, introduce yourself to your neighbors. You don't have to like them, but do make it easy for them to like *you*. Interested neighbors are the best way to avoid (or at least to minimize damage from) break-ins, vandalism, fire, unauthorized parties, and anything else that can ravage your home while you're away.

Tips for Tipping in the 'Hood

When the holidays roll around or it's simply time to support
your local scout troop, be a good neighbor and patron. You'll
reap the rewards in better service and neighborly relations.

- If you're happy with your mail service and want to reward a
  job well done, why not bake a batch of holiday cookies for
  your mail carrier?

- Give a holiday tip to your paper deliverer—especially if he
  or she is still a kid on a bike. A few extra few bills in an
  envelope around the holidays is all that's needed to show
  your gratitude.

- Holiday treats or tips for your doorman or building superin-
  tendent are also much appreciated and go a long way toward
  service with a smile.

- Support (or at least be kind to) your local scout troops. Be
  polite to any neighborhood child who knocks on your door,
  even if you can't donate to his or her cause.

Keeping Up Appearances

It *does* matter what your neighbors think.

You've broken the ice and become socially invested with your neighbors, but Girl Scout cookies alone won't get you respect. Be a good neighbor by maintaining the upkeep of your front yard, driveway, and sidewalk (or, if you live in an apartment complex, choosing tasteful window coverings, not bed sheets), and observe proper etiquette while you do it.

DAD SAYS: "Don't be neglectful—be considerate."

1. Clean oil stains off your driveway and curbside parking spots. Many parked cars (especially older and vintage models) tend to drip oil. Over days and weeks, this oil will form sticky, unsightly black blots on the concrete and irritate the heck out of neat-freak neighbors. Don't try to wash the spots off with soap and water. Cover all of the spots with a generous amount of sawdust or cat litter, and the oil should be completely lifted within a day or two. Discard the litter or sawdust. For extremely thick stains, repeat the process with new dust or litter until the area is clean.

2. Take in your garbage and recycling cans as soon as they're emptied. At the curb, they're taking up valuable parking space, which is unforgivable if you live in the city.

3. Don't park derelict cars (or boats) in your driveway. Nothing looks trashier—or decreases morale (not to mention property values) faster—than a junk car on permanent display.

4. Complete home improvement projects during daytime hours only. Banging hammers and squealing power tools are the last thing your neighbors want to hear when they're trying to sleep. Pack the loud stuff in after seven in the evening, and keep it quiet until eight in the morning.

5. Have loud, late parties infrequently, if ever (never on weekdays), and warn your neighbors at least one day in advance. Everyone has a right to celebrate, but this does not mean celebrating the start of every weekend.

6. Clean up your own detritus. Lawn clippings, fallen leaves, and leftover bits of projects should never be swept or blown onto your neighbor's property. Bag your trash, and deposit it neatly in your own garbage or recycling bins.

7. Don't sneak excess trash into your neighbors' bins. Chances are, they've got enough garbage to fill them.

8. Be gracious when accepting gifts, and give freely to your neighbors in return. Share fresh fruit from your trees or produce from your garden whenever it comes into season—without expecting your neighbors to reciprocate.

Tip Keep fences at the back and on both sides of your property in good repair and looking pretty—don't wait for your neighbor to take the initiative. Set sagging fences upright, fix holes on your own, and save your receipts for materials. When you're finished, ask your neighbors if they'd like to pay for half of the expenses—but don't take them to court if they demur. Remember, you're doing this for your own peace of mind.

Lawn Care Made Easy

 Keep it green!

You don't need a green thumb to have a beautiful yard, but you do need to wrap your own thumbs around some basic tools and machines regularly. It takes effort to maintain the health of your front- and backyard greenery, but it takes a lot more effort (and usually a painful financial infusion) to heal it once it starts to die from neglect. Learn to love the process, not just the results.

DAD SAYS: "When it comes to lawn care, there's no middle ground."

1. Water your lawn in the early morning, so that the moisture soaks in before the hot sun causes it to evaporate. Don't water at night; you'll only foster the healthy growth of snails, slugs, and other night crawlers.

2. Adapt your watering schedule to changes in climate. Under average conditions, you should water your lawn once or twice a week. If temperatures soar over 80 degrees Fahrenheit (26°C) and stay there, you'll have to water every other day to keep the grass hydrated. During rainy periods, either suspend watering or reduce frequency to once every other week.

3. To revive a brown lawn, spray it with a standard weed and feed

compound (available at your local nursery or supermarket garden aisle, along with a hand-cranked or power spreader) and water every day until it recovers.

4. Spray your lawn with feed once per season if it's heavily trafficked, or twice a year if it's rarely stepped on.

Tip Don't overwater when there's a drought. Many cities have passed water-rationing ordinances that go into effect during recognized periods of drought. You can actually be fined for watering under such conditions, so keep up with the news and be a good citizen.

5. Mow your lawn once a week with a hand or power mower. Let the size of your lawn determine your arsenal of lawn-care tools. Don't invest in power mowers (or weeders or blowers) unless your lawn is larger than 100 square feet (9 square m) and you have a place to store them.

Tip **If you're investing in a power mower, consider models that mulch as they mow. Cut grass is finely chopped and redistributed on the lawn as mulch, instead of requiring disposal.**

---

6. Edge your lawn whenever you mow it. Use a hand or power edger (or weed whacker) to clean up stray tufts around flowerbeds and walkways.

7. Nip weeds in the bud. Regular treatments of weeding and feeding keep weeds down to a manageable level, but a few stubborn weeds always survive. Pull these die-hards out by hand (root and all), or use a manual weed-pulling tool (which goes about a foot [30 cm] into the ground and makes it easy to collect the whole plant). Always keep pets inside while you're spraying.

8. Keep snails and slugs down by killing them (i.e., salting or squashing) when you see them. Do not use slug or snail bait if you have pets or if your yard is frequented by wildlife—it is extremely toxic.

Mow, Mow, Mow Your Lawn

Allow your grass's growing rate to dictate your mowing schedule. When the grass is a little less then double the recommended height, it's time to mow. Mow less often during drier months, so your grass has time to grow longer roots (which are more resistant to heat). Be sure to wear long pants, closed shoes, and eye protection when you mow.

1. Drag your mower onto a flat surface to check and/or set the blade height. For bentgrass and Bermuda grass, use a ½-inch (1.3-cm) or 1-inch (2.5-cm) setting; for bluegrass or ryegrass, use up to 2½ inches (6.3 cm); for zoysiagrass, use 1½ inches (3.8 cm). Ask your nursery specialist or consult your mower's manufacturer guide to determine proper settings for other varieties.

2. Run your mower back and forth in straight lines, parallel to the wall of your house.

3. Use your weight to keep the mower properly balanced as you mow up and down hills. Press down slightly as you mow uphill, to keep the mower's nose from grounding; mow slowly when you go downhill, so the front end doesn't lift.

4. Be careful of rocks. If you mow a hidden rock that's just the right size, your mower can spit it in any direction—which can hurt. Rocks can also hurt your mower and make it less efficient.

5. Dispose of your clippings in a designated compost bin.

The Science of Shoveling Snow

Make sure your winter wonderland doesn't keep you from getting where you need to go.

Winter is beautiful, especially when it snows, but if it keeps on snowing, you'll have to leave off beaming for a while and get out your trusty shovel. Snow management is never one of Dad's favorite chores, but it's a must if you want to get into and out of your house with ease.

DAD SAYS: "Dress in layers so that you're warm—and mobile."

1. Choose a shovel with a wide blade that allows you to pitch the snow easily off the end or to the side, and make doubly sure that it isn't too heavy. Many shovels have specially designed

handles that distribute the weight evenly, so that you don't have to provide as much "heave" from your back muscles.

2. Keep your feet set about hip-width apart, your knees bent slightly, and hold the shovel close to your body.

3. Scoop a shovelful of snow and toss it forward and to the side of your projected path. Do not twist or bend your back as you toss the snow. Continue to clear a path from your house to the street by shoveling the snow forward and to the sides.

4. If the pavement is covered by a layer of ice, chip the ice away with your shovel blade.

5. Salt the walkways and driveway with rock salt to keep the ice from reforming during the night. (In a pinch, you can also use sand or cat litter.)

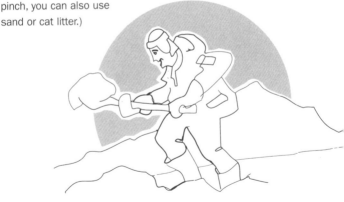

Don't Neglect Your Downspouts

Keep a lid on roof maintenance.

Clear your downspouts and gutters as frequently as the weather requires, but at least once in the autumn, while the leaves are still falling and before the winter cold sets in, and once in the spring, when windswept leaves and debris can clog gutters. Windy or stormy conditions will cause leaves and detritus to pile up more quickly.

DAD SAYS: "Take care of your foundation by starting at the top."

1. If the design of your house allows you to climb safely onto the roof, use your 8-foot (2.4-m) ladder to do so. It's much easier to walk back and forth along the gutters as you work, instead of climbing up and down repeatedly. If your house has a pitched roof, however, rooftop maneuvering isn't an option.

2. Get a sturdy plastic bucket for the gutter debris and a buddy who will stand below you and empty your bucket when it's full.

3. Put on a pair of cloth work gloves, so you won't catch your fingers on metal edges or sharp bits of flotsam. Keep chalk (or a roll of colored tape) in your pocket, and mark the spots where roof tiles will need further maintenance.

4. Extend your ladder, and rest it against the house—not on the gutter—at the corner closest to the downspout. U-shaped aluminum bars that bolt to the ladder (available at hardware stores) are the best way to keep your ladder at the appropriate attitude.

5. With your scoop or bucket, begin removing debris from the top of the downspout, and then work your way along the gutter. As your bucket gets full, hand it down to your buddy.

6. Check the integrity of gutters, roof tiles, etc., as you work; straighten bent gutter hangers, and mark spots that merit scrutiny.

7. Use your garden hose to give the whole drainage system a final flush; note any leaks, and caulk them with acrylic latex caulk.

8. Make sure that your downspout is pointing away from your foundation: Water should be directed away from the edge of your house to prevent flooding and sliding.

9. If your gutters don't have screens already (and you live in a high-wind or weather-prone area), consider installing them; you can do it yourself, and they'll cut your maintenance needs in half.

Barbecue Basics

 Nothing compares to food cooked on an open grill.

Dad is—and always will be—the czar of backyard grilling. With tongs in one hand and a fork in the other (and serious stains on his "Kiss the Chef" apron), Dad delights all comers with new twists on old staples, including top-secret marinades that Mom would love to get her hands on. These recipes are the keys to his kingdom.

DAD SAYS: "Fire up the coals, and butter up the chef!"

To start, you need to gear up with the right equipment.

1. Choose your grill. Barbecues come in many shapes, sizes, and price points. Don't purchase more grill than you need. If you're planning to use the grill on a balcony or deck or in a small backyard, get a little hibachi instead of a big, looming console. If you opt for a charcoal grill, you may be exposed to more carcinogens than with a gas model. The characteristic flavor of a charcoal grill cannot be duplicated by a gas grill, however.

2. Purchase a special set of long-handled grilling utensils, including metal tongs, a spatula, a two-pronged fork, and a set of skewers. Never use plastic utensils on a grill.

3. Invest in a pair of fireproof gloves or mittens.

4. Any brand of coal will do. Some types produce more pleasant-smelling smoke, but they rarely improve the flavor of your food.

Now you're ready to fire it up.

1. Based on the amount of food you're planning to grill, fill your barbecue with coals (more food requires more coals).

2. Arrange the coals according to your cooking needs. If you're cooking only one dish that doesn't require searing, create a uniform, level pile. Otherwise, bank the coals higher on one side of the grill to create a high-temp area for searing and a low- to medium-temp area for general grilling and roasting.

3. Squirt a generous amount of lighter fluid directly onto the coals. Remember not to set the fluid canister right next to the grill when you light it—otherwise, your barbecue (and you) could explode.

4. Use an extra-long match or lighter to light the coals; keep your face turned away so you don't singe your eyebrows.

5. Wait for the coals to heat up; _never_ add more lighter fluid. Impatience can result in a dangerous surge of flame.

6. In case of leaping flames or grease fires, cover the grill or close the vents to smother the fire. Don't panic. Just remember that fire needs oxygen to burn, and you're the one in control of the air.

Tip | **Never reheat or reuse your coals. Once they're used, they're useless. Let them burn down completely before disposing, so you don't start a fire in your garbage can.**

---

7. The coals are ready for action once they've stopped flaming and turn slightly ashen or gray. This will eliminate the oily or chemical taste in grilled dishes.

8. Heat the treats. Chicken, steak, hamburgers, hot dogs, pork, seafood, and veggies all taste wonderful when cooked on the grill, but each food on your menu will require a different cooking time:

Chicken: 12 to 15 minutes a side
Hamburger and steak: 3 to 7 minutes a side, depending on thickness and desired doneness
Hot dogs: 4 to 5 minutes a side
Pork: 8 to 10 minutes a side, depending on thickness
Fish: 3 to 7 minutes a side, depending on thickness
Shellfish: 5 to 10 minutes a side, depending on size

Dad's Backyard Masterpieces

It's all in the wrist—and the recipes.

Here are a few of Dad's favorite grillers, guaranteed to thrill taste-buds on every tongue. You'll want to stick with the china when you serve these dishes; they're a far cry from paper-plate fare.

DAD SAYS: "Prepare for a feast for the senses."

SHRIMP SKEWERS, THAI STYLE

2 cups (475 ml) unsweetened coconut milk

1 "squirt" green curry paste (or to taste)

1 shallot, chopped

1 large garlic clove, chopped

1 pound (450 g) jumbo shrimp, cleaned

1. Combine coconut milk, curry paste, shallot, and garlic in a large bowl.
2. Add cleaned shrimp, cover, and marinate in the refrigerator for at least 2 hours.
3. Skewer shrimp and cook on a medium-hot grill for approximately 2 minutes per side, or until shrimp turn opaque.

Serves 4

TOP SECRET TRI-TIP

1 cup (240 ml) Italian dressing

2 heaping tablespoons (30 ml) Dijon mustard

2 cloves pressed/minced garlic

1 shallot

1 beef tri-tip

1. Combine marinade ingredients in a bowl.
2. Submerge tri-tip, and cover; marinate overnight in the refrigerator (or no less than 3 hours).
3. Sear tri-tip on the hottest part of the grill for 5 minutes per side, and remove to the medium-hot area for final cooking. Do not overcook!

Serves 4

 Tip Substitute portabella mushrooms for the tri-tip to make a hearty vegetarian entree. Grill approximately 10 minutes a side.

MEISTER BURGERS

1 pound (450 g) beef, turkey, or game meat, ground to order

4 dashes Worcestershire sauce

2 tablespoons (30 ml) soy sauce

Salt and pepper to taste

1. Combine all ingredients in a large bowl.
2. Form into patties approximately ¾ inch (1.9 cm) thick and 5 inches (13 cm) in diameter.
3. Grill on medium heat until done to perfection.

Serves 4

VEGGIE MIGHT SKEWERS

Assorted vegetables (cherry tomatoes, onion, peppers,
mushrooms) in bite-size pieces
Salt and pepper to taste

1. Precook dense vegetables like peppers, onions, carrots, and others on the grill or on the stovetop before skewering with other fast-cooking veggies for grilltop finishing.
2. Thread skewers by alternating veggie flavors and colors: one tomato, one onion quarter, one pepper chunk, one mushroom, for example.
3. Place on the grill with skewer handles positioned clear of the grill area.
4. Grill on medium heat, turning frequently, until done.

Make 2 to 4 skewers per person

CALAMARI STEAKS

Salt and pepper to taste

Fresh calamari steaks (the flat body, not the tentacles)

Fresh lime juice

1/4 cup (60 ml) honey mustard or 1/4 cup (60 ml) marinara sauce

1. Salt and pepper each steak, then squeeze a whole lime wedge over each.
2. Grill on low to medium heat for approximately 3 minutes per side. The outside of each steak should be firm, while the inside remains soft. Do not overcook. Calamari is best when it's nearly raw.
3. Serve with heated honey mustard or marinara sauce for dipping.

Serve 1 to 2 steaks per person

BRICK CHICKEN

6 chicken pieces (breasts, thighs, or butterflied small birds)

Top Secret marinade (see recipe on page 137)

Salt and ground peppercorns to taste

6 foil-wrapped bricks

1. Marinate the chicken for several hours in the refrigerator, and add salt and pepper to taste.

2. Place each chicken piece on medium-hot grill, and weight each piece with a foil-wrapped brick to facilitate even cooking and absorption of marinade.
3. Cook 10 to 20 minutes per side, or until done.

Serves 4

HONEY MUSTARD PORK CHOPS

2 cups (480 ml) honey (or Dijon) mustard
2 tablespoons (30 ml) honey
2 tablespoons (30 ml) barbecue sauce
1 teaspoon (5 ml) wasabi powder (or paste)
1 chopped shallot
½ clove chopped garlic
Salt and pepper to taste
4 extra-thick (¾ inch [2 cm]) pork chops
Jellied cranberries

1. Combine honey mustard, honey, barbecue sauce, wasabi powder, shallot, and garlic in large bowl or Pyrex dish. Add salt and pepper to taste.
2. Add the pork chops to the marinade, and marinate in the refrigerator overnight.
3. Grill on medium heat for approximately 10 minutes per side, or until done. Do not overcook.

4. Serve with jellied cranberries.

Serves 4

GRILLED EGGPLANT

1 large eggplant

Salt

½ cup (120 ml) marinara sauce

1. Slice eggplant into ½-inch (1.3-cm) thick steaks.
2. Salt liberally, and allow to sit (on a plate or board) for at least an hour. This removes the bitter flavors.
3. Grill at medium heat for 5 to 10 minutes per side, or until done, and serve with heated marinara sauce.

Serves 2 to 4

GARLIC EVERYTHING BUTTER

1 whole head garlic

¼ cup (60 ml) olive oil

Salt and pepper to taste

½ teaspoon (2.5 ml) fresh tarragon

1 teaspoon (5 ml) fresh rosemary

1 teaspoon (5 ml) crushed red pepper flakes

¼ stick (28 g) softened butter

1. Cut the head off the top of the garlic bulb.
2. Pour a liberal amount of olive oil directly onto the garlic, then add the herbs and spices.
3. Seal the bulb in foil, and grill it (upright) for 45 minutes.
4. Unwrap the foil, and squeeze the softened, spiced garlic cloves into the softened butter. Mix well; if a thinner texture is desired, add olive oil.

Serves 2 to 4

 Tip

Spread garlic butter on French bread halves, and broil to make garlic bread, or use it as a zingy gourmet condiment on toasted hot dog and burger buns.

UNEXPECTED APPLES
½ stick (56 g) softened butter
1½ cups (360 ml) brown sugar
1 cup (240 ml) chopped walnuts or pecans
1 tablespoon (15 ml) cinnamon
1 teaspoon (5 ml) nutmeg
1 squeezed lime wedge
6 large apples, any variety

1. Combine the butter, sugar, nuts, spices, and lime juice in a medium-size bowl.
2. Core the apples, and fill with the nutty mixture, lightly coating the skin as well.
3. Wrap the apples in foil and set them upright on the grill—before you cook dinner.
4. Keep the apples cooking on the side or in a corner for approximately 1 hour, while you cook the rest of the meal.
5. Unwrap the apples for a surprise dessert. Serve with banana- or praline-flavored ice cream.

Serves 2 to 4

How to Host an Outdoor Party

If you really want to follow in Dad's footsteps, pay attention to how he hosts a barbecue.

· Before the party, stock several ice chests with ice and beverages. Make sure that there are plenty of plates and napkins.

· Prep food before your guests arrive, and keep it refrigerated until it's needed.

· Sport a decorative apron and flamboyant hat, so everyone knows whom to compliment.

· Don't start grilling until your party is complete: let your guests nibble at vegetable platters or chips and salsa until everyone arrives, so no one is left out of the main event.

· Don't hover around the grill while you wait for the coals to heat up. Unless you're preventing small children from poking their fingers into the fire, this is your time to mingle and enjoy your own party. Refresh your guests' drinks, or direct them to the ice chests for refills.

· Don't serve people one at a time; set out platters of barbecued chicken, burgers, etc. (along with condiments and utensils), and invite guests to help themselves.

· When you've finished grilling, clean the barbecue and move it aside as soon as the coals burn down to allow people more room to mingle and play.

CHAPTER 6:

Dad on Success

According to Dad, things were different in his day. Work was harder, hours were longer, wages were smaller, and, by gum, he was more grateful for less. But the basic strategies for professional and social success remain the same: Talk the right talk, and walk the right walk in the right shoes—and make sure you're stepping in the right direction, whether in the workplace or on the dating scene.

Fortunately, when it comes to setting a goal and attaining it, no one has better advice than Dad. He's canny, careful, and cool—and the more you learn, the cooler he gets.

Always Dress for Success

 Put your best foot forward when you apply for a job—and remember to shine your shoes.

Jobs aren't won or lost on talent alone. Like it or not, your appearance—from your personal style to your grooming habits—can either convince employers that you're right for the job or give them an excuse to dismiss you.

The key here isn't making a *good* impression; it's making the *right* one. If you're interviewing in a corporate office, for instance, the style should be crisp, tailored, and professional. A business suit (including a tie for men) is preferable.

DAD SAYS: "Wear a suit!"

SUITABILITY (FOR WOMEN)

1. Stick with a dress or skirt cut to knee or mid-calf length, or well-tailored pants, paired with a blouse or shell and jacket. Whatever style you decide to wear, make sure that it fits you well. Remember that clingy dresses lack business cred.

2. If you're unused to wearing the shoes your outfit goes with, practice walking in them before the interview. Clomping, shuffling, and mincing painfully will not present you to your best advantage.

3. Choose a suit in nonsynthetic fabrics whenever possible. Polyester, nylon, and acetate can cause you to perspire.

SUITABILITY (FOR MEN)

1. Nine and a half times out of ten, a suit is the most appropriate thing to wear on an interview, and it's not ever *in*appropriate.

2. Your suit should be conservatively tailored and made of a tightly woven, matte fabric. Loose weaves—think linen—tend to wrinkle and stretch out of shape; synthetic fabrics often have

a telltale, used-car-salesman kind of sheen. You do *not* want to be that guy.

3. The jacket should not be too tight or too wide across the shoulders, and the pants should be neither wide-legged nor too long.

4. When the jacket is buttoned, you should be able to lift your arms without the seams becoming ominously tight across

your back and without the front gaping open. At the same time, the top of the jacket should fit snugly, so that the shoulder seam does not drop below your natural shoulder or stick out too much.

5. The sleeves should be short enough to allow about half of the shirt cuffs to show below them—if your sleeves are too long, you'll look as if you're borrowing someone else's suit.

6. Hem your pants or have them professionally hemmed at the right length. Most retail stores can complete alterations at little or no charge, and dry cleaners generally offer alteration services. The front of the pant leg should completely cover your shoe lacings, with a slight "break"—not a bag—in the leg line where it rests on the top of the shoe.

Tie Tying for Beginners

Nothing says "professional" better than a tasteful tie.

Unless they're absolutely sure that the prospective employer favors business casual (or ripped hip) attire, men should wear a tie to their interviews. Just follow these steps, and you'll be tying a half-Windsor on in no time.

Dad Says: "You've learned it before—now learn it for real."

1. Choose a tie that isn't too wide or too bulky to knot easily.

2. Button your shirt to the neck, and lift the shirt collar.

3. Drape the tie around your neck. It should hang unevenly, with the wide end about twice as long as the thin end.

4. Cross the wide end over the thin end (about 3 inches [7.5 cm] below your chin), and wrap it around the thin end twice.

5. After you make the second wrap, bring the wide end up through the neck.

6. Tuck the wide end through the front loop, to complete the knot.

7. Gently pull down on both ends to tighten the knot, then grasp the thin end to slide the finished knot up to your neck.

8. Flip your collar back down, and fasten your tiepin (if you have one).

Close Shaves

First impressions are often correct.

If you can't find time to shave before your interview, your prospective employer can make a pretty accurate assumption that you'll come to work late, fail to proofread reports, and lose your PDA on a regular basis. In other words, you've *already* lost the job. Always use a straight razor or an electric shaver to give a final polish to your professional look.

DAD SAYS: "If you want to be clean-cut, be clean—and cut!"

1. Give yourself time for a proper shave.

2. Use a new blade (or new razor).

3. Steam your face to open your pores. Wet a washcloth in very hot water, and hold it to your face until your skin begins to flush.

4. Squirt a generous amount of your favorite shaving cream into your hand, and apply a thick lather to your face.

5. Fill the sink with warm water, or leave a trickle running from your faucet. Wet your razor, and begin shaving—against the direction of hair growth. Use your free hand to pull the skin taut when necessary, to lift each hair into the path of the razor.

6. Rinse the shaving cream and hair from your razor after every two or three strokes; very thick shaving cream will probably need to be rinsed after every stroke.

7. Check around your ears, under your jaw line, and around your nose to make sure that you haven't missed any hairs.

8. Treat any nicks or cuts with a styptic pencil (or blot them with tissue) to stop the bleeding.

9. Use aftershave, astringent toner, or an aloe-based gel to clean and soothe your pores.

10. Rinse your razor completely, drain the sink, and wipe out the hairs and soap scum.

Ironing Basics

  Always iron your shirt and slacks.

Your suit should never look as if it's been napped in, nor should it ever actually be napped in. Take the time to do the job right, so you press out the old wrinkles without pressing in new ones. Use an ironing board (free-standing or tabletop) for best results. Heat the iron to the appropriate setting depending on the fabric to be ironed: cool for synthetics, hot for cotton garments. Give the iron time to fully come to temperature before beginning.

DAD SAYS: "A wrinkled suit is just de-pressed—so that makes ironing cheap therapy."

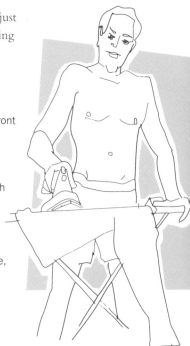

TO IRON YOUR SHIRT:

1. Iron the back and then the front of the collar.

2. Iron cuffs next (inside first).

3. Lay sleeves flat, and smooth out any creases, then iron them on both sides (back side first).

4. Iron front panels one at a time, from shoulder to hem.

5. Turn the shirt over to iron the back of the shirt.

6. Your shirt will be slightly damp when you're finished, so hang it immediately to avoid further wrinkling.

TO IRON YOUR PANTS:

1. Turn your pants inside out.

2. Iron the waistband, pockets (both sides), and fly, then turn the pants right-side out.

3. On the pointed end of your ironing board, iron the outside of the waistband and pleats (fit the pointed end into each pleat in order to fill it and smooth it out).

4. Lay the pants lengthwise on the ironing board, with any permanent creases lined up. Fold the top leg up to reveal the inside of the bottom leg, then press the bottom leg.

5. Turn the pants over, and repeat the process for the second leg.

6. Move the bottom leg aside, and fold the top down so you can press the outside. Repeat for the second leg.

7. Fold the pants carefully over a suit hanger (or hang them from the waistband with clothespins) to prevent them from becoming de-pressed again.

Get a Job!

 A good résumé combines honesty with a little spin and spit and polish.

Your résumé shouldn't seek to change who you are, but it should display you to your best advantage. No matter how extensive your work history or your skills may be, always keep your résumé to a single page. Add a focused, concise cover letter, and you're sure to make it to the interview round.

DAD SAYS: "Make sure your résumé makes it to the top of the pile."

1. Keep your résumé concise and informative. Don't let your design flair overwhelm the page. Information should always be the primary focus. Include your contact information: home address, home phone number, cell phone number, and e-mail address. Make it easy for employers to reach you immediately. Tailor your work history to match the stated needs of each job you apply for.

2. Include an enthusiastic cover letter. Like your résumé, your cover letter should be concise and customized in style and content to suit the needs of each prospective job. Your language should be simple, professional, and approachable. Outline who you are and

list your top two or three most applicable qualifications. State your interest in learning more about the open position in an interview, and list the most reliable times or ways to contact you.

3. Ace the interview. Dad's biggest rule? Don't be late! Nothing is more disrespectful and disappointing than a prospective employee who can't get to an interview on time—it hints at a long career of lateness to come. Dress appropriately in neat, conservative clothing (and clean shoes). Greet your interviewer with a firm handshake and appropriate eye contact. Be courteous and engaging—and follow the interview tips on the following page.

Tip

When you arrive for the interview, bring another copy of your résumé with references attached on a separate page. You'll be prepared in the event your interviewer wants to pass your résumé on to other colleagues within the company.

Dad's Best Interview Tips

- When potential employers first contact you after reviewing your résumé and cover letter, be flexible with your time—if they only have one or two available time slots in which to interview you, try to accommodate them. Don't put them off until the following week or even further; they might just find the "perfect" person before they've even met you.

- Walk the walk. When you meet your interviewer, make sure your body language conveys confidence. Train yourself out of nervous habits such as smoothing or playing with your hair, tapping your fingers, scratching a nonexistent itch, or sucking your teeth. When you're offered a chair, sit comfortably and don't slouch. Do not wiggle your foot up and down if you cross your legs. And don't forget to shake hands again at the end of the interview.

- Talk the talk. Don't try to take control of the conversation. It's good to show that you're interested in the company by asking questions, but wait for your prospective employer to set the pace. Be forthcoming with your answers.

- Be flexible and creative in your negotiations. If you really want the job but your potential employer says there simply is no give on the salary, agree to an initial lower salary, but propose that your employer give you a salary review six months after you begin the job. Just remember to get every negotiation point you've agreed to in writing. A smile and a handshake only go so far.

Get the Raise You Deserve

 Get paid what you're worth!

A busy boss doesn't have time to keep tabs on your daily productivity. He or she almost certainly doesn't know exactly what you do, have done, and will continue to do that's wonderful enough to deserve a raise. So when it comes to asking for a raise, state your case as a clear, simple summary of facts instead of justifying your merit by singing your own praises. Don't debate or argue, *clarify*.

DAD SAYS: "Make the most of opportunity."

1. Before asking for a raise, take an honest look at your performance, and verify that a raise is deserved. From your boss's point of view, you must be pulling your own weight to deserve an increase.

2. Pick a good time to make your request. Don't ask for a meeting if you're disgruntled, unhappy, or in trouble. Wait until your work has been praiseworthy and your attendance record is spotless: You'll be putting your best foot forward because you can be confident about your performance.

3. Once your review has been set, come prepared with any documentation or information that could be relevant and helpful to your case.

4. During your meeting, maintain eye contact—and don't roll your eyes, even if you get angry or bored during the conversation. Above all, don't interrupt.

5. If the answer is no, extend the timetable. Suggest that your boss commit to a future review and a future date for your raise to go into effect. If nothing else, this will guarantee that the issue will be revisited in a later conversation.

6. Be appropriately grateful for any increase your boss grants you—without being obsequious or fawning. The more professional and direct you are, the more you will be perceived as a professional deserving respect.

> *Tip*
>
> Remember: No one is indispensable. Sure, you take work home. Sure, you're loyal. You're practically family! But would the company fail without you? Brace yourself: The answer is no. Don't get complacent and become a problem child because you think your boss must recognize the flawless quality of your work. The bottom line is what counts in the end.

Dating Prep According to Dad

 Anything can happen on a date, so pack your wallet or purse and car for contingencies.

When you realize that Dad's automatic answer to (almost) every dating question is "NO!" you'll know how lucky you are to be getting any sensible advice at all. After all, Dad's primary mission in this department is to keep you safe. And mission number two is to smooth your path, wherever possible, through the rocky terrain of social protocol. Follow the advice below, and if things still don't work out . . . well, ask your mother.

DAD SAYS: "Prepare for the worst; prepare for the best."

Your complete dating kit should include the following:

1. Enough cash to cover dinner, a movie, and other planned expenses, plus a little extra for emergencies. If your credit limit is a wing and a car payment away from your current balance, feel free to rely on the plastic. Just remember that those diabolical finance charges and surprise fees can take you near or over your limit before you know it, and an expensive restaurant—on a date—is not the best place to be when you find out.

2. Personal identification. If you're going to be driving, don't leave your license in your other pants or purse. The night you forget your license will be the night you get pulled over. Even if you don't plan to drive, it's best to bring proof of your age and a picture I.D. for whatever contingency.

3. Extra car key. Unless you keep a spare key in a magnetic box on your car's chassis, you'll be in a pickle if you lock the keys inside your car.

4. Contraceptives. Don't rely on your date to be responsible. Take control of your own future, and bring your own.

5. Cell phone. In a real emergency, you can call Dad.

Dad's Dating Dos and Don'ts

 Chivalry and dating etiquette are not dead.

Good manners, in the modern age, aren't nearly as dogmatic or silly as they once were, but there are still a few classic dos and don'ts that bear consideration. An action that seems considerate to one person can seem downright rude to another, so keep your ears open and your radar on, and get ready to run the gauntlet.

DAD SAYS: "Be aware of the rules of engagement."

1. Don't be late. For the anxious person who's waiting for you, there's no such thing as "fashionably late." Being punctual shows you to your best advantage: mature, respectful, cool, and collected.

2. Don't twiddle your thumbs. If you're waiting for your date at his family's house, be pleasant and make conversation with his family until he appears. Be interested, but not too curious; be funny, but not offensive; and above all, don't look at your watch.

3. Orthodox chivalry may be outmoded, but when in doubt, err on the side of thoughtfulness. If you're the driver, unlock the passenger door for your date before getting into the car yourself. And if you're the passenger, it doesn't hurt to lean across the seat to unlock the driver's door.

4. Be sure to clean your car in advance. It's all well and good to be yourself, but keep some of yourself to yourself for at least the first few dates—until your partner is besotted enough to overlook some (mild) untidiness.

5. If parking is an issue in your restaurant's neighborhood, do use the valet option if it's offered. There's nothing more frustrating than driving around and around, watching other people nab spots on the other side of the street while fate giggles and tickles your temper.

> **Tip** If you've got money to burn on this date, be polite, and pass your valet a generous gratuity when he or she gets into your car. This increases the likelihood that your car will be parked in a close, accessible, and reasonably well-lit spot and that it will promptly appear when you call for it.

6. If you definitely want to see your date again, pay the check. If you definitely *don't* want to see your date again, pay the check. (It's faster than trying to figure out how to split it, and you don't want to hear, "Put it on your card, and I'll give you the cash later.")

Restaurant Etiquette

 Whether on a date or dining alone, always be polite but firm to the waitstaff.

There's a fine line between being assertive and being over-bearing; there's a similarly fine line between an overworked waiter and a neglectful one. When you receive poor service while you're on a date, how should you handle it? If you complain or chastise the waiter, everyone is embarrassed, and no one is happy. But if you don't seize the reins in some manner, you and your date will have to put up with long, apologetic waits and feelings of inadequacy.

DAD SAYS: "Attention paid is a gratuity earned."

1. If your waiter seems to be ignoring you, keep an eye out, and flag him or her down by raising a hand.

2. If you can't get noticed, flag down another waiter and pass on the message that you'd like some service now.

3. When you speak to your surly waiter, do not apologize for requiring special attention. You're simply expecting him or her to be a waiter. Make it clear that your time is not unlimited and that you would be grateful for your waiter's efforts to expedite service.

4. If all else fails, speak to the powers that be. Excuse yourself and ask the maitre d' to page the restaurant manager. Outline your difficulty. If your service has been truly abysmal, a good manager will offer some kind of compensation. If this is an isolated occurrence in a familiar restaurant or a first experience in a restaurant that you'd like to try again, don't burn your bridges by throwing a tantrum or causing a memorable scene. Simply remain calm and reasonable.

5. Finally, remember that you do not need to reward poor service. If you remain dissatisfied with the treatment you've received, you need only leave a nominal tip.

Tipping Tips

 Tipping is an art all its own.

The average tip for good service has increased to just under 20 percent over the past decade. Remember: Undertipping (unless the service has been noticeably poor) will not impress anyone, whether you're on a date or out with friends.

DAD SAYS: "It's important to know whom to tip and whom not to tip."

1. Do tip the waitstaff; don't tip your maitre d'.

2. Do tip your parking valet for bringing your car back in one piece.

3. In hotels, do tip your bellhop; don't tip the concierge. Always, always tip the housekeeping staff. (A good rule of thumb is to leave 2 percent of your total bill for each night of your stay.)

4. Do tip your food delivery person; don't add a tip to the total when you pick up your own takeaway order.

5. Do tip barbers/stylists (unless your stylist happens also to be the owner of the establishment, in which case no tip is needed); don't tip dry cleaners.

Banking on Dad: Your Intro to Finance

Dad is not a bank—but you can bank on his advice.

Follow Dad's guidelines to smart money management, and you'll stay happy, wealthy, and wise—without bankrupting

Dad in the process. First, you have to shake hands with your bank balance and get to know its cycle of ups and downs.

DAD SAYS: "Budgeting is the key to a positive balance."

Ask yourself a few simple questions, and jot down the answers:

1. How much, on average, do you earn in a month—*after* taxes? Include any and all regular income from side jobs or freelance work, but do not include bonuses, birthday gifts, gambling gains, or windfalls.

2. How much do you spend on rent (or mortgage)?

3. How much do you spend on utilities during an average month? Try to use the totals from spring or autumn bills, when the weather was moderate, to make your estimate.

4. How much do you spend per month on transportation? Include the costs of gasoline, tolls, transit passes, and parking.

5. How much do you spend on telecommunication and media services during an average month? Total the monthly charges for phone, cable, and Internet services.

6. How much do you spend on necessities? (Brace yourself: that does *not* mean sushi.) Limit your list to basic household

must-haves such as groceries, home maintenance supplies, toiletries, and health remedies (don't forget daily medications and regularly refilled prescriptions, if any).

7. How much per month do you spend on insurance? Include the cost of your health and automotive plans (unless they're part of your employee benefits package), along with renter's or home-owner's insurance and any other plan that you carry.

8. How much per month do you spend on healthy recreation? Include membership fees for gyms or health clubs, plus monthly dues and/or supplies for social and/or hobby clubs.

Now add up your answers to questions 2 though 8, and subtract the total from your monthly income. The resulting number is your *discretionary* income. This is how much you can spend on vices—including luxury sundries (such as beer or wine), luxury habits (such as dining out or going to bars or nightclubs), and luxury items (such as high-tech toys and complicated shoes)—or virtues, such as investments and retirement plans.

Remember that planning for the future doesn't require you to become a different person, but it does require honesty. Identify your expensive habits, and assess their value. Then divide them into two groups: one for stuff that truly fulfills you and the other for the take-it-or-leave-it stuff that you tend to do without thinking. Cut out the extraneous things, and commit to the pastimes that feel important; call them justified expenses, and deduct them from your discretionary income.

| *Tip* | Never put old bank statements and credit offers in the garbage or recycling bin. Use a shredder to destroy outdated financial records, along with any printed material that refers to your social security or driver's license numbers. |

Are You Ready to Invest?

 Now that you've figured out your budget and spending patterns, it's time to start planning for the future.

If your discretionary income is less than 10 percent of your monthly net income, you are living hand to mouth or spending your entire paycheck during the period before your next payday. You need to reassess your current spending habits before you can begin to think about long-term investments. (In fact, your first step should be building a savings cushion for the sorts of sporadic maintenance costs or single emergencies that can instantly erase your discretionary income.)

But if your discretionary income is between 10 and 25 percent of your monthly net income, you need to read up on your investment options and start the ball rolling.

DAD SAYS: "Put 10 percent of your income into a savings or investment plan every month."

1. First, begin saving for retirement. The sooner you put money away, the more your contributions will grow—and you're never too young to think about getting old. If possible, enroll in your company's retirement program.

2. Think about other investment possibilities. Read up on the stock market and on personal money management before committing your funds. With a limited income to play with, you have virtually no money to burn.

3. Set a clear goal before investing a penny. Are you aiming for short-term gains—such as accruing the capital to buy a car or put a down payment on a house—or for long-term security? Determine your patience level. This will help you chart an investment strategy, whether it's a high-risk, high-yield plan with quick returns or a more conservative, steady growth.

Credit Appeal

If you want to buy a house, a yacht, a car, or virtually any other big-ticket item, you'll have to secure a loan or qualify for a finance plan.

- Make yourself attractive to lenders by making regular, timely payments on an outstanding debt—such as a college loan, which carries low interest and can be periodically refinanced—or on the balance of at least two credit cards.

- A good credit rating requires a good credit pattern. You have to owe money to demonstrate your ability to pay it back and thereby impress someone else. At the same time, you don't want to be eaten alive by interest charges, so pay off your high-rate credit cards immediately, every month (or as soon as possible), and reduce your loan payments to the minimum in order to do so.

4. Put your monthly 10 percent into the stock market if you want to see a quick return on your investment. It all depends on your strategy. Buy conservatively in big names and stable companies, and you're likely to see a slow but reliable growth in the value of your stock.

   - Buy into new technologies or initial public offerings, and you will either see rapid growth and short-term profit or an epic crash and burn.

- The market's big names are reliable picks for long-term growth, but they don't come cheap—each share is quite expensive with respect to the rest of the market. Your money will grow (and grow more, if you make a bigger initial investment), but it won't grow in leaps and bounds.

- It's a lot more fun (and just as smart in the long run) to buy shares in companies that produce the products you actually use: If you like these goods, you can generally bet that millions of other people do, too. Buy stock in companies that cater to your own interests, and you'll feel a real connection to your portfolio.

- Watch the headlines. Look for global trends or health issues, and buy stocks in the companies that produce innovative goods and pharmaceutical solutions. Use common sense. It doesn't take an insider's knowledge to know which way the wind is blowing—just stay alert!

- Be patient. Keep your money in the market for the long haul, through downturns and even crashes, and your temporary losses will be offset by overall long-term growth.

Index

Acknowledgments

Through the vicissitudes of life and the writing process, Dina Fayer and Dr. Robert Fayer (the real Pocket Dad) remain the best of friends and coconspirators. The talented team at Quirk Books has, once again, pulled a happy rabbit out of a rather battered hat. A special thank you must go out to Mindy Brown, our editor. For support and contributions throughout the years, we'd also like to thank Roger Reinitz (electrician and handyman par excellence); LaRece Egli (for reminding us that campgrounds have latrines); Jane Sumner (for everything); Toshi, Imelda, Aleks, and Melody "Mel-Mel" Chan-Doss (along with Lucy, Bev, and Sharman Spector) at Britex; Dina Bloom (for investigating strategies); Annette and Al Stolberg; Blanche and Sandy Weltman; Will Shortz of the *New York Times* crossword (for daily brain massage), and, of course, Maude Fayer: Pocket Mom and genius.